charles@afghanistan

charles@ afghanistan

CRAZY ENCOUNTERS FROM THE NOT-SO FRONT LINES

CHARLES McDONALD HOLT

Vantage Point Books and the Vantage Point Books colophon are registered trademarks of Vantage Press, Inc.
FIRST EDITION: August 2011

Published by Vantage Point Books
Vantage Press, Inc.
419 Park Avenue South
New York, NY 10016
www.vantagepointbooks.com

Manufactured in the United States of America
ISBN: 978-1-936467-02-0

Library of Congress Cataloging-in-Publication data are on file.
0987654321

Cover design by Michael Fusco.

acknowledgments

As far as acknowledgments go there are just too many people to risk hurting feelings. Instead of trying to list a bunch of names only to find I missed one after it was too late. I chose to name but very few. I love and respect all of the people that encouraged me to write my stories and I hope you enjoy seeing them in print.

Thank you God, and his name is Jesus, thank you for keeping your hand upon me while I was in a strange land among a people that would have my head.

Thank you to our Troops of the United States of America.

Roxane . . . I love you!

Brandy Briggs, James Guidry, Robert 'Button' McDonald, I love you.

Now to the one person I cannot group with anyone else. I have great respect for and owe so much to my friend John Allison. We served in the US Coast Guard together for years and have remained friends till this day.

John, the effort you went through to push me to write was incredible. This book is as much yours as it is mine and Roxane's. You encouraged, I wrote; you edited, I corrected; Rox will collect the royalty . . . we are as one.

Thank you, my friend.

Charles McDonald Holt, a.k.a. Tex

contents

INTRODUCTION   xi

1. The Application Process   1
2. Getting Ready to Leave   9
3. I'm Outta Here   17
4. London to Dubai   20
5. Dubai, The Hotel Room   23
6. The Naked Man   26
7. The Modern-Day Foxhole   29
8. Naked Revenge   31
9. Overbearing?   33
10. Air Afghanistan   35
11. In Country!   39
12. Bathroom, Head, Latrine   44
13. Our Village   53
14. Dining Facility, aka DIFAC   60
15. Can You Trust Your Friends?   63

16. Post Exchange, aka PX   65

17. City Inside   67

18. There Is a Hole in the Roof   69

19. Reality Check   72

20. Mortar Fire   75

21. My New Job; Driver-Heavy Truck   77

22. The Camel Spider   80

23. Safe Inside the Gates   83

24. I Put My Foot in My Mouth . . . Again   85

25. The Polish Soldier   87

26. The War: It's Real   90

27. My Own Truck   92

28. My Afghani Helpers   94

29. Land Mines   97

30. Attacked!   100

31. The Mammut   102

32. Attacked Again!   104

33. Wrong Email   106

34. The Fishing Story   108

35. Hot and Sandy   112

36. Upgraded   115

37. Sharing My Lunch   118

38. The Flight Line   122

39. Big Problem   126

40. FBI – CIA   129

41. The Prison That Does Not Exist   130

42. Black Water?   132

43. Rocket Attack   134

44. Popal & Broder   136

45. The French and Their Uniforms   140

46. Red Cross   143

47. The $120 Haircut   144

48. Home for a Time   151

49. Frankfurt, Germany, Gate B-20   153

50. Red Cross Again   160

51. Fallen Comrade Flag   162

52. The Final Chapter, Thank You   164

introduction

What initially began as a few emails to friends has turned into an ongoing documentary.

My wife, Roxane, and I had just come home to Texas, after being on tour with some well-known Broadway musicals for the last three years. I would like to say we were part of the show, singing and dancing, but I can't. Rox could probably pull it off but not this fat boy.

We owned one of the trucks it took to move these shows from city to city. It was great fun until tragedy struck. First we had a major engine malfunction to the tune of $38,000.00 – let me tell you that hurt. We spent a lot of time and money in the selection and purchase of a new truck. Almost immediately upon our purchase my wife's stepdad passed away, another tragedy. I found myself on tour without my helpmate because she went to be with her mother. I did not like it one bit.

I found myself in a strange truck by myself, and I felt

as lost as a man could feel. I did the only thing a man of my higher learning could be expected to do in a time of crisis like that—I quit my job and sold my truck! I know, I'm a wuss. But it seemed like a good idea at the time.

I soon found out I didn't have the money it took to live a normal life without a job so, I started looking for work. My dad used to tell me the only problem he ever had with looking for work is that he always found it, and I think I have the same curse.

I was hired to go to Afghanistan and drive a truck for the US Military. I wrote an email to my friends to let them all know what I was doing, then followed up that email with others, just to keep everybody up to date.

What started as a note to friends has turned into the journal you are about to read. This journal really has no specific intent, other than to share with my friends what this old Texas boy (not really old, just a figure of speech) was experiencing, outside the confines of the southeast Texas piney woods.

As I rewrite all of my emails, I will try to take away from the email format by combining each story as gracefully as I can for your enjoyment. All of the original stories are here in their entirety, many are untouched in the way they read. In some, however, I have gone more in depth and expanded upon the original material.

You will discover I begin a lot of my paragraphs with the word "I". A simple explanation is the fact that I am talking about me. What can I say? I hope you enjoy my story.

CMH

charles@afghanistan

1

the application process

Hello, everyone, I am about to embark upon another adventure. This one may well turn out to be one of the most memorable ones for me. l will try to keep those of you that are interested up to date in my progress toward Afghanistan.

I joined the US Army in 1983, and then took what is called an Interservice Transfer to the US Coast Guard. I'm telling you this to give you an idea of the process I had to go through in order to secure the job in Afghanistan, as a contract worker. Let me tell you, it is easier to join the military, and there's much less paperwork involved.

The first thing I had to do was upload my resume over the Internet and fill out an online application. It seemed like it was an easy enough process—no hassles. Then about two weeks later I received a call from the company's recruiting department. That's when the real hiring process started.

1. The first thing I had to endure was a long interview over the phone. I was excited when the call first started. The recruiter was telling me as much as he could about my projected assignment, and in a way it seemed like he was trying to scare me into not taking the job. He kept reminding me that this was going to be dangerous in so many ways. People may shoot at me; there might be roadside bombs, suicide bombs, landmines, etc. The scariest part was the fact that any serious medical help would be thousands of miles away.

   The recruiter could not dissuade me. I convinced him that I did understand I was going to be in harm's way by traveling to Iraq or Afghanistan to work. The only alternative was to stay home with my wife. What choice did I really have? You married guys will understand.

2. A time was set to join a conference call that same night. I dialed in with an access code and joined about twenty people already on the line with more checking in all the time. This was pretty cool if you remember the party lines when you were a kid. The most we had on our line as a kid were four other families. This was the same thing times five.

   As each person checked in from their personal telephones, they would introduce a little piece of their everyday lives and the cacophony that goes with it. I needed the quietest and most secluded place I could find in my Man-Cave. "The Bathroom." No noises to give away my presence except the turning of a

newspaper page and maybe the occasional . . . Well
you get the picture. This is where all the important
decisions in my life are made (most of which are
later appealed by my wife).

There were a whole range of conversations
going on in the background as we were all waiting
for the recruiter to join in. Kids were crying, dogs
were barking, traffic noise from someone who must
have been driving a New York City cab filtered in,
and there was even someone working a cash register while talking to customers. Wow! This was
not at all professional in my opinion and when the
recruiter finally joined us at the exact moment he
said he would, he must have agreed with me.

With all the noise going on in the background I
almost missed him when he came on the line. The
recruiter started out in a calm, professional voice
explaining he was about to call out each person's
name to ensure that everyone was present and
accounted for.

It started with the first few people almost missing
the roll call because of the noise. As the roll call
continued, the recruiter started raising his voice and
I could hear the aggravation growing in him.

Finally a downright mad fellow told everybody
to shut up and listen—give the crying baby to
whomever it is you are shouting at and ask them
to leave the room. Kick the dog outside or give
up your lazy-boy to the dog and you go outside,
and whoever is in traffic, pull over and roll up the
dadgum window so everybody else can hear.

Then somewhere in the back of my secluded location I hear a quiet knock and a soft voice . . . " Honey, are you OK? Charles, who are you shouting at? Who is in there with you?" The rules for my Man Cave are very clear, so when I didn't answer, that small voice trailed off in the distance muttering something I'm sure I don't want to write down.

OK,OK,OK, said the recruiter, it is part of the hiring process to endure a conference call that will last about forty-five minutes. Those of you who cannot treat this conference call as a personal and professional part of the process need to hang up.

Most of the noise died away. Everybody knows what a dog being punted sounds like immediately, followed by a sliding glass patio door. The baby suddenly quieted. Hopefully the dog and the baby lived in different households.

Finally the roll call was over and the forty-five-minute ordeal came to a close. The whole thing consisted of my phone interview all over again. The conference call is just a restatement of the danger involved in this kind of work and an effort to weed out anyone who may not be a serious candidate.

The best part came at the end. Another roll call, which the recruiter failed to tell any of us about. Several people had not stayed on the line till the end for some reason or another and were struck from the hire list.

3. The interview and conference call were just the beginning. Most of the process was done via the

Internet. After the conference call I received an email from KBR with two Internet links.

The first one took me to a whole different dimension of employer application forms. This included work history, medical history, family history, and on and on. Of course you can't stop once you get started.

The email gave instructions on exactly what information was needed before I started working on this modern, state-of-the-art, computerized, easier-for-everyone-involved, Internet-based application system.

About two hours into filling this thing out I realized that just maybe I should have read those directions more closely. Maybe I should have read them the first time.

I decided to go on and work with the other link in the email and come back to this one later because I didn't have the information I needed to complete it. No big deal, right?

The second hyperlink, as it is called, took me to another company's Web page so I could give them all the vital information needed to do a thorough background check on me. I hear people saying how worried they are about putting such personal information over the Internet for fear of identity theft.

Please, someone steal my identity! I could at least forward all the Canadian-based bill collectors' early Sunday-morning collection calls to them. What a way to get around the Do Not Call List— hire someone in Canada to do it.

The background checking website was fairly painless. Now all I have to wait is about ten days for the information to come in. Am I a criminal? I don't know yet. We have to wait for at least ten more days.

Now it's time to collect the information from my briefcase in order to finish this modern, state-of-the-art, computerized, easier-for-everyone-involved, Internet-based application system.

"Your Internet session has expired due to no activity." "Please log in with your user identification and the unique password you created when starting this session."

Aaaaaaaaaaahhhhhh!!!!!!!

You guessed it. If you don't sit down with everything you need to complete this modern, state-of-the-art, computerized, easier-for-everyone-involved, Internet-based application system, it will shut off without saving your information.

This is a good time to take a break from writing. I find my mental disposition heading south just remembering this little snag concerning the modern, state-of-the-art, computerized, easier-for-everyone-involved, Internet-based application system.

4. The next day I received an overnight package with all kinds of forms to fill out. Medical release forms, insurance forms, next-of-kin and power of attorney forms . . . All kinds of stuff. Also included in the package was the identical employer application form that had caused me so much grief.

The instructions said to fill it out and bring it to Houston with me at the time I was scheduled for orientation. I filled it out, yes with many cramps to the hand, but I wasn't going to be caught NOT following instructions again.

5. The doctor visits were quite easy although time consuming. My family doctor—I will call her Dr. Blahey (mainly because that is her name)—is very easy to look at. My wife never reads what I write so I can say this without much fear of retribution, and by making sure that none of her friends gets a copy of this book.

   If the copy you have says in the Authors Bio section at the end of the book, "Charles is survived by,"or, "In Memory Of . . . ,"well, I guess she did actually read something I wrote after all.

Dr. Blahey was able to give me the six-month scripts for my medication as required to go to Iraq or Afghanistan along with a medical release saying I probably wouldn't die from the lack of medical needs for at least six months unless I stopped breathing for an extended period of time.

The release from the dentist saying I would not need dental care for at least six months was more of a headache. A tooth that might need a root canal almost cost me an all-expenses-paid vacation to an exclusive infidel resort at the base of the Himalayas.

I had to convince the dentist that I could not afford the surgery without insurance and I was not going to have insurance unless I was hired by the company that sent me to him. I swore to him that when I returned and had insurance, if he thought I still needed the root canal, he could do it.

I no longer have that tooth and it only cost me $80 to have it pulled. I am a proud Texan after all, and to a certain extent teeth are an optional accessory.

I've given you the five steps to take if you want to go to work in another country, and I'm pretty sure this will be the basic procedure that every company employs.

2

getting ready to leave

I arrived in Houston to process for KBR . . . that's Kellogg, Brown & Root for you laymen. It was supposed to be a week long orientation and then fly out at the beginning of April, but alas here I am almost a month later and just now leaving. I can't even promise I'm leaving until the wheels of the airplane come off the ground here in Houston.

I learned Sudafed elevates your blood pressure. I'm sure everybody that reads this will already know that little tidbit of information, but I had to learn it the hard way. I was taking Sudafed for sinus congestion the day I took my physical and I failed the blood pressure check. In a few short words I was sent home until I could provide documentation from my family doctor, "Dr. Blahey," that it was a fluke or that my blood pressure is now controlled by medication. So I have had a long wait.

I made it to Houston for the second time and hope to complete the orientation this go-around.

I will be brief in my description of how hectic this part was for me because I did not title my story Charles in Houston or Charles on His Way to Afghanistan—as my wonderful bride reminded me after she proof-read (yes I said she proof-read) my story up to this point. It was her very own words I added . . . "In Memory of." At least I got to eat supper before that little bout.

The place I was instructed to go to was secret. I'm not kidding. I arrived at the hotel (one of eight in the area) that the company used for new employees to stay in during orientation.

Somehow a suite on the top floor had been reserved for me. It was a high-rise hotel and very nice. The view from my balcony offered a panoramic vision of downtown Houston that was incredible. A view somewhat like you would find on a postcard. I looked down and wow! A rooftop swimming pool on a lower level of the hotel, right below my balcony. That's all the time I am allowed for describing my accommodations. Or of the additional views I enjoyed from there.

We all ate breakfast in the hotel lobby and then headed outside to wait for a bus to arrive and pick us up.

The orientation center was located on the backside of a mall. Not some strip mall or shopping center but a full-blown mall where people of my financial means just go to sit and watch other people. Malls can be very entertaining.

I said it was secret. How can our meeting place be kept secret right in the middle of swarms of people visiting the mall, you ask? It's actually pretty easy.

There are no signs to point the way. There is no banner hanging over the doors. When someone drives around looking for a parking spot they never go to the back, and if they did, all they would see is a section that appears to be closed down.

From inside the mall when people come up against a closed gate or a passage that is blocked they just steer away from the obstacle. In other words the people inside are herded around the area occupied by the orientation center and are none the wiser.

Everyone at the center was given an ID badge and a color-coded lanyard to wear while inside, and we were instructed to take it off before leaving the building. The colors are changed each week so it is easy to identify what group you arrived with and where you should be if a security guard or instructor caught you wandering around.

As each of us made his entrance to the back of the mall, we were met by security and had to swipe our ID badges. It did not matter if you walked out to get some sun or smoke a cigarette, you didn't come back in without logging back in. Every class had a scanning machine to swipe your card and if you missed it within a few minutes someone would call your name over a loudspeaker, embarrassing me . . . er, I mean anybody . . . who failed to log in.

At any given time you could swipe your card and a computer screen would let you know your status in the orientation process and where you had to be next. It would let you know if your assignment had been changed or if you were ready to ship out. Pretty cool, but we were rats in a maze . . . just like the folks on the other side of the wall shopping.

We all had many classes to attend and the group of people I was going through orientation with were as diverse as they come. There were people from all over the United States as well other countries. The pay scale for Americans was much higher than others, but the cost of living made up the difference.

One of the classes we had to go through was a chemical and biological attack scenario. The buddy system is the only way to pass this part. At the sound of the gas alert (not the same gas alert sound I was used to) we had to grab a yellow slicker suit with rubber boots and a gas mask.

After putting the gas mask on, we then had to put on the suit and rubber boots. The buddy system comes in here with a roll of duct tape. The first one suited up would grab someone else and help them, then take the duct tape and tape all the areas around the neck, face, wrist, and ankles. We even taped the button seam down the front and then looked for any tears in the suit.

This was all kind of fun and a relief to get out of a regular classroom setting, but how much of it was really going to help? We were inside an air-conditioned mall and everyone knows how cold those things are. I was sweating like a pig and ready to pass out from the effort. Just think what it would be like in the desert. I can see it now . . . This is a drill, this is a drill. Gas!

Gas! Gas! . . . This was a drill. All clear! All clear! All clear! Where is Charles? I can tell you . . . Charles is lying in a heap out in the sand somewhere looking a lot like a two hundred- pound lump of salt taffy.

The last thing of note was the fact that we all had to undergo another physical conducted by the company at another secret location. Yes, I said secret again. We were all loaded onto a bus and taken to another facility near the Houston Ship Channel. Once again this place was fenced off with guards and nothing to identify it from the outside. Anyone looking at it from the street would see what appeared to be an abandoned ware-house, but once you got on the inside it was a total transformation.

Inside the warehouse a whole complex of mobile trailers were set up with different stations for doctors and nurses to perform the entire set of tasks involved with having to go through a physical. This is where we all received the many shots that are required to work abroad. I received seven shots in all and gave about a gallon of blood. I should say they took the blood because I sure didn't want to give it them, at least not that much. The most amazing thing is we didn't have to wait six months for the results; it can actually be done in just a few minutes if the doctor wants it.

OK, I'm here for one last night in the luxurious Wyndham Hotel and Resorts eating high on the hog, but by this time next week I'm going to be eating next to a bunch of people that think the more you stink the manlier you are. Pray for me because I am a clean freak and like my showers but I guess I will have to learn to scrub with a handful of sand now, and if I want to blend in with the crowd I will have to buddy up with an extra-smelly camel or something.

I don't think it will be that bad really but I will try to create a more accurate picture of my life over there next time. So far it is just speculation.

If I told you I was not a little apprehensive I would be lying to you. Everyone that is going into Iraq or Afghanistan for the first time is scared because you don't really know what to expect. You can tell someone till you are blue in the face about your own experiences but that counts for nothing when it comes down to another person's challenge of meeting the circumstances. In fact I am scared to death but have too much pride to back out now.

My assignment has not changed. I was hired to go to Afghanistan, but there is always the possibility that I might be needed in Iraq. With the troops starting to leave Iraq and heading to Afghanistan, the contractor jobs are moved there as well.

If you are curious about where the military is planning to beef up their presence, all you have to do is find out where the contract labor force is headed.

I remember when I was in the army we drove our own trucks and cooked our own meals, but times have changed. I am thankful to have a job that will allow me to help in the support of our troops, but I also believe it would be better if Uncle Sam took all of this big money being spent for contract labor and increased the servicemen's pay and benefits and allow them to do it themselves.

We have all been warned that, although our troops are grateful for the service we are going to provide, there are also going to be hard feelings over the difference in pay. For example, a soldier driving a truck in Afghanistan may be making $30,000 a year and a contractor doing the same thing will be earning around $100,000.

If it becomes unbearable for whatever reason the contractor can just quit and come home, but our troops cannot.

OK, we have come to the end of our stay in Houston; we all have our orders, plane tickets, and a $500 advance on our first paycheck. Believe it or not, the advance was given to us right before we boarded the plane. Its purpose is in case anyone one gets into trouble while entering any of the countries we will pass through on our way to Afghanistan.

I don't know what kind of access I will have to the Internet and phone service. When I am actually in the country and learn what I can do as far as getting information out, I will send that info in the generic form to everybody. If you don't care, "delete it". If you don't want to hear from me, just drop me a line saying so and I will in turn send you a nasty computer virus that my buddy Ron let me play with for about a week.

If more information is desired of your hero (me), check with my beautiful bride, Roxane. Her email is rox-cha@juno.com. Make sure you put "My Hero" in the subject line. I'm just kidding. If you did that she may send you an update about George Clooney. It would be safer just to ask about me.

Wish me luck, and those who have a direct link to God, remember to mention my name and remember my family. Thanks for taking the time to read my mail and I'm not even telling you to send it to five of your friends or you will have a string of bad luck.

Those of you who want to respond, please do so. I will be glad to see anything in my mailbox besides spam when I get a chance to get it.

Talk to ya'll later,

Charles

3

I'm outta here

Well, this is my first update. I am not sure when I can send it, but I thought I would write it as I am experiencing it right now.

I boarded the plane at 3:15 p.m. today and took flight at 4:00 p.m. For anybody who has ever flown on a plane like this it won't be a big deal to you, but this is my first.

My experiences in flying consist of a few jet rides in the eighties just locally and a few c-130 military planes and a bunch of helicopters. Just this year alone I have flown three times . . . well, this one being the fourth time.

The first two I thought were big planes but the last one was small enough that all it did was follow the interstate from Houston to Beaumont, Texas. This last flight scared me to death and I had no desire to ever fly again. The plane would leap up and then free fall like a roller coaster that just wouldn't quit. To make matters worse I was sitting next to a guy who said, "You know why this plane has two engines?" I fell into his trap by asking him why. He said, "If one of the engines fails, the second one will carry us all the way to the crash site." I told him not to talk to me for the rest of the trip.

This plane has not scared me yet. This plane is so big I did not even know it was taxiing out to the runway till I looked out the window. When it took off there was a bit of concern, I suppose, but it was quiet and there wasn't much movement except in the pit of my stomach when I saw the ground falling away.

Let's see, this plane has two rows of seats on the left, three rows in the middle, and two rows on the right. I am fortunate enough to be by the window on the left side but unfortunate enough that my neighbor felt comfortable enough to remove his boots. The first half of this flight is nine hours and forty-five minutes, and we still have six hours to go . . . wheee, and I mean, I wish he would put his boots back on.

Enough of that; the cool thing is every seat has a TV monitor in the headrest with eight channels to choose from in a variety of languages. I mainly stick to the English language, believe it or not.

The coolest part is one of the channels shows a live map where the plane is tracking across the sky. I can see the states and cities we pass over and it continually gives temperature, altitude, and ground speed. We just crossed the Eastern Seaboard and are just getting over the Atlantic. Our altitude is 35,000 feet, averaging 600 mph, and the outside temperature is below zero Fahrenheit. I also have an electrical outlet to plug in my computer. There is a phone in my armrest that I could use if I wanted to use a credit card and mortgage a kidney.

The time zone I'm going to be in is nine and a half hours ahead of central time. It sounds like a mistake but it's not. If it is twelve noon in Houston, it will be 9:30 p.m. in Bagram, Afghanistan.

Well, good people, I think I'm going to find some tissue to stuff up my nose and watch a movie. More to come when I can.

Charles

4

london to dubai

This is a continuation of my trip to Afghanistan. I know that it will most likely go out at the same time as the first, but I don't have Internet access to send them out as I write.

The first plane took us into Gatwick Airport, London. I would like to tell you about all the neat places I visited while in London but I think everyone is familiar with the Universal Airport Restroom.

About the only thing that I experienced with Gatwick is the extensive walking. I'm used to airports like Dallas, which has a train to take you from one plane to another. Not so here.

Gatwick has the moving sidewalks, which I thought were cool but I found I was in the way. I wanted to ride them and everybody else wanted to walk on them. What a waste of human energy. Why build the sidewalk that does the work for you if you are still going to have to go through the effort of walking anyway? I guess my way of thinking is the reason I'm as fat and out of shape as I am.

Nothing really remarkable about the airport in London so I will move on to describe the plane we were going to ride from London to Dubai.

As we were coming to the end of our ten-mile hike/ride of the sidewalks, I could see the airplane. From what I could see, the paint looked to be peeling off the outside of the plane and it did not look to be as new and safe or comfortable as the Continental flight I had taken from Houston.

From the looks of the outside I was expecting the inside to be worse. I was really surprised to be seated in a very clean and much cooler environment (temperature-wise) than the last plane. I have described how nice the Continental flight had been with the TV screen and all, but I have to say this one was an upgraded version.

I was sitting in my seat, and it felt like I was sitting inside a video game at a game room. The monitor was mounted into the headrest like the last one, but this one was a touch screen with about twenty movie channels and news stations to watch. It also had many regular TV shows to choose from, but guess what? Not all of them were in English.

Oh yeah, the thing had all sorts of games just like Nintendo, which was a bit out of my realm of expertise. I did play and I'm proud to say I won a game of Hangman but I did lose a fair share of victims before I won, but hey, I did manage to save one guy.

The coolest feature was the outside camera system. Everybody had a view of a forward-looking camera from the front of the plane to show us the same view the pilot had and we also had a view from a camera looking straight down. This is way better than trying to look at the ground out the window where the one with the window seat is the only one with a view.

I don't need to describe the view, but it was what made the flight so easy. It was a distraction for me to be able to sit there and see where I thought the pilot might need my opinion, and believe me, when he came in to land and I saw the plane did not line up on the runway just right, I offered my opinion. I'm not sure they will let me fly with them again but it was nice while it lasted.

The worst part of all of it was the length of time it took to get to Dubai. It took nine and a half hours from Houston to London and seven hours from London to Dubai.

I will write about my stay in Dubai next time. Till then I hope everyone is doing well and thanks for the responses I have gotten from some of you. You know who you are and you are going to stay at the top of my favorite-people list. As for the rest . . . well, if you're even getting this email that means you're at the top, too.

Take care,
Charles

5

dubai, the hotel room

I want to tell you about Dubai. Most of you have seen the History Channel and have seen stories about Dubai.

As we departed the plane, it started to sink in real quick—we're not in Kansas anymore, Toto.

After clearing customs (which was not fun) we all got separated in the crowd. I was as lost as could be until I spotted another fellow that looked lost and followed him. I don't know how we made it to the baggage claim area, but we did.

Someone was there to meet us and herd us onto a hotel shuttle. The ride was unremarkable except it seemed like everyone was driving a BMW or Mercedes. I can only guess these cars are cheaper here or everyone wants to keep up with the Joneses. You either have a luxury sedan or a moped and not much in between.

Dubai is where they built the Palm Islands by dredging the sand from the sea floor and kept piling it up until they had formed man-made islands. Very rich people then bought these islands and built mansions and resorts. Dubai is now building the World Islands and also boasts the tallest luxury hotel in the world. This is a very rich country.

As we approached the hotel through city streets that looked like they were getting into some rough areas, we became concerned. The buildings are about twelve to fourteen stories and they are all housing in this area. Every balcony had clothes hanging out to dry and all the windows were open for ventilation. It is very warm and humid.

We were all a little worried that we were going to a hotel with no air-conditioning and that we may have to fight our way inside.

We were wrong to worry so much because this is a very nice place. The hotel is actually a four-star hotel right in the middle of some one-quarter- star housing. The buildings look just like on the TV, go figure.

This is completely different from any hotel I have ever been in. I was assigned a room and got an electronic card key to open the door just like everywhere else I've ever been so I thought I was set.

I took the elevator that could only carry four people at a time. There were two elevators and the sign inside claimed an eight-person maximum, but that did not apply to Americans.

The combined weight of the group I am being transported with from the States could hold their own in a tug-of-war with an aircraft carrier. Three people per elevator may be pushing it.

From what I understand, most fat guys coming over are recognized as fresh meat because of the bulk around the belly. I'm fresh meat and don't look forward to sweating it off, but I'm here now, so bring on the furnace.

6

the naked man

OK, I made it to the seventh floor, found my room, and was definitely ready for a shower and bed. Thirty-six hours with the same socks on is a bit much for me.

I used my card key and the door unlocked just like back home in the States, and what did I find? There was a naked man standing on the other side of the door . . . yep. I closed the door and checked my room number again and sure enough this guy was in my room. I guess you could say since he was naked that it was his room.

Now I remembered they told us we would have roommates, but I'd forgotten. I knocked on the door and opened it again. This time the naked fellow was across the room shucking on his pants and then rushed across the room to shake my hand and greet me.

In the most elegant southern style I could muster, I refused to shake the hand that I just knew needed to be attacked with vigor by a bar of soap, antibacterial soap, bleach, battery acid. I wasn't rude but that hand was not going to touch me in any kind of greeting.

That was just the beginning of my experience with this room, the most uncomfortable and weird, but still just the beginning.

No I didn't, so don't even go there . . . I had my own bed.

As I walked in, there was a row of switches on the wall and I noticed the guy's card key was inserted into a slot beside these switches. I thought it was just a place to hold your card and didn't think about it.

The first thing I wanted to do was plug in my computer so I could send out email. There were no plugs I could use. This hotel room is wired 220. You could plug in a clothes dryer but I didn't have one of those, I had a laptop computer.

I called downstairs for help and they hung up on me. Maybe it is the language barrier or something but rude is rude and I have a very low tolerance level for rude people. The concierge met me at the door with a smile on his face as I was walking out of my room to check on our phone connection problem.

After demonstrating to the concierge what I wanted to do with the funny little plug for my computer, he produced a convertor for me. I suspect he knew what I wanted the whole time but didn't quite let it show till a $5 bill enlightened him. He was happy. I was, too, till breakfast when I learned what the exchange rate was. I had given him the equivalent of $18.

I have been here only one day and I went half a block from the hotel with a group to eat at an outside diner.

Remember when I said Dubai was very rich? Well they are, but the wealth did not spread to this diner.

Don't get me wrong, I thought the food was excellent. I don't know what I ate but there were big hunks of meat hanging from the rafter just off the sidewalk (hopefully it never had a driver's license) and a guy stripped the meat off, rolled it into what I know as a tortilla (unleavened bread), and directed me to eat it.

If you get another email from me in the near future, you will know I survived.

7

the modern-day foxhole

I have to describe the bathroom. I know I sound like the country boy who came to town, but a bathroom is what makes a hotel livable.

The first thing I noticed is the entire bathroom, floor, wall, and countertop were all marble with a large drain in the floor.

I thought it was very nice and would be easy to clean by washing the water into the drain. To make this an easy task I saw a water hose with a hand-held faucet. The kind that we have in the kitchen sink—you pull the hose out, press the button for a rinse. It was mounted between the toilet and the tub. I thought, how efficient.

The toilet does not have a handle. I had to study this a bit because I did not want to have the concierge coming back just to help me leave the bathroom in the same pristine condition I had found it. I would figure this out on my own.

I finally found a fancy little button mounted into the wall. It wasn't hard to see, it just wasn't where I thought it should be. I found it just in time because I had already turned my attention to hunting for a scoop. This is one time I was not proud that everything is bigger in Texas.

The shower . . . oooohhh, the much-needed shower. No hot water.

What can you say about a four-star hotel that hides the flush button and has a water hose in the wall of an all marble bathroom? A hotel that had already surprised me with a tiny elevator and my very own naked man? Why did I expect to have hot water?

The water was cold but I got in anyway. I thought that just maybe everybody was taking a bath at the same time. For my needs cold water worked just as good in one-tenth of the time.

Oh yeah, remember the hose and the marble floor with the drain? Yeah, while I was showering, the water backed up from the drain.

I got out of my cold shower and stepped into a large puddle of cold water and bits of toilet paper. I jumped back in the shower, attacked my foot with soap, and then grabbed the hose from the wall where it was conveniently mounted between the toilet and shower.

Imagine a soldier in a foxhole. I'm in the tub with my water pistol trying to shoot the bits of paper back into the drain. Now I understand why this hotel did not qualify for a fifth star.

8

naked revenge

Skip forward to bedtime. I couldn't find the switch to turn my lamp off—you have got to be kidding me. I decided to explore the row of switches on the wall by the front door.

There was a switch for the TV, and every light had its own switch, the bathroom having three switches just for the lights in there. I had one too many switches on the wall. Like with the toilet, I was determined to figure this out myself.

I could see writing on this switch but I had to get my flashlight out in order to see it. I'd already turned on seventeen lights in the room but none were shining where I needed it. The tiny letters stated very clearly when enough light came into play that this switch turned on the water heater.

I'm tired of writing so I'm going to explain the neatest part about this room. Remember the card holder next to the water heater switch?

It does more than just hold the card. You have to insert this card into the slot to make the switches work. Without this card no lights, no water heater and no air conditioning. Not even the clothes dryer plugs work.

My naked guy got up and left the room taking the air conditioning controlling card with him. I woke up in a sweat. You think I got upset because he didn't tell me I needed to put my card in the slot to make the cold air keep working? YES!!!

I didn't say anything to him, in good old Texas consideration for my naked man; I let him take another cold shower before he flew back to London. I have the room to myself now and when the steam from my shower clears out, I will continue getting ready for my flight.

9

overbearing?

This was not supposed to be a running commentary, but I have had some time on my hands . . . so for now that is what it has turned into. I don't intend to keep it up, I promise.

When I get to the military base I'm going to tonight, I won't be able to elaborate as much because we were all warned, all computer activities will be monitored and all phone calls will be listened in on by the military for security purposes.

It may sound overbearing but an example was given about a contractor (like me) that gave up too much information and the army sent him back home. I have no idea if he was charged with a crime.

This guy was asleep when mortar shells dropped into the camp. The next day he posted a Google Earth map on his MySpace page and placed a mark showing his friends where the men slept and showed another mark showing where the mortars fell, and went on to explain that if the enemy had just been another one hundred yards or so in another direction a lot of men would have been injured.

Granted, he was elaborating on the conditions he was experiencing and just meant to share this frightening episode with his friends, but guess what? The bad guys now know where to drop the next bomb because they also know how to use the Internet. I would like to think the Taliban are not very sophisticated or computer savvy but they have to be somewhat intelligent or we wouldn't be in a war with them.

I'm going in at night because the night gives a little added protection. The bad guys may know how to use the Internet, but they can't see in the dark like the US Military can.

I will write again as soon as I can find an Internet signal in Afghanistan.

Charles

10

air afghanistan

I don't know if I made the right decision by coming to Afghanistan . . .

My experience so far has had enough latitude to allow for my dry sense of humor, but right now, that humor fails me.

I won't go into details about this place until I'm certain I can describe it without violating any security regulations, but I will try and paint as good a picture as I can.

The airlift out of Dubai was not fun. The flight from Houston to London was nice and the flight from London to Dubai was even better. The flight from Dubai to Bagram, Afghanistan, was more like Air America in Vietnam.

I'm not trying to be funny when I describe the plane as reminding me of the overloaded buses in South America that have more livestock than people. The seat I was sitting in was broken in the small of the back and my tray table was hanging on by one hinge, and I'm being serious.

The first part of the flight was uncomfortable because of the seat and being crowded, but I was feeling OK. The plane was obviously serviceable or it wouldn't be in the air. It was the required combat flying after we got into Afghan airspace that put me off the whole flying thing.

While we were above the clouds it wasn't so bad, but then we started to descend into some clouds that from the top were a beautiful heavenly white, but the lower we dropped the darker the clouds and the more turbulence.

The plane started to be tossed around like it was a toy and then to make matters worse the pilot started his combat landing procedure. This is where he would speed up and slow down, zigzag and do many maneuvers to make his flight as unpredictable as possible to anybody that might want to shoot at us from the ground.

He would put us in a sudden nosedive and then bank real hard in one direction and then another. When we came to our landing zone it seemed to me that the pilot just put the plane into a nosedive to drop as fast as he could to the landing field.

This flight into a war zone was truly the first thing that made the whole thing real to me. I am going to call the flight Air Afghanistan from now on.

It sounds like I'm complaining but I don't mean to because I am proud we made a safe landing. It was, however, among the most frightening things I have ever experienced. I don't know if I was the only sissy onboard or not. I was too busy worrying about myself.

I think when I leave this place I am going to walk to the nearest coastline and hop a freighter back home.

Where we landed is at an altitude similar to Denver, Colorado, which means thin air that is hard to breathe. I have been plagued with breathing problems for the last five months so this just makes it even harder.

I was trying my best not to show my discomfort but in fact I felt like I was going to go into a serious panic and embarrass myself. If I could have called my wife I'm sure I would have just quit on the spot and had them send me home.

I certainly don't feel threatened here because the military controls this area, but I was having trouble breathing. I don't care how tough a man is, when you take his air supply away from him he will turn into a little girl crying for her mama.

I did calm down, but I think I know where my determination came from. It is the fact of being stuck here. The quickest I could possibly expect to leave would be several days away.

If I had let this beat me and told them I wanted to go home they would let me, but by the time I left I would have become acclimated to the area and high altitude with no need to go home. I would have shamed myself. Don't get me wrong, I may quit tomorrow but for now I think I will be OK.

I know a big factor is the jet lag and lack of sleep. In the last eighty-six hours I have had about six hours of sleep. I slept in Houston last Tuesday night. My day started at 5:00 a.m. Wednesday morning. I flew out of Houston at 4:00 p.m. Wednesday and landed in London nine hours later. We had a two-hour layover and then a seven-hour flight to Dubai. After crossing about eight time zones I was able to sleep for about six hours Thursday night in Dubai because we left at midnight on Friday to go on to Afghanistan.

After arriving in Afghanistan we spent till noon on Saturday being led around by our new captors. Captors may not be the right word for it since this is a self-imposed detention in a war-torn country. No matter how I say it, I was not just going to be able to walk home at the end of the day.

11

in country!

I finally got to go to bed. In a tent about a hundred feet long with fifty other guys on cots. A tent does not do much more than block the direct sunlight. In the daytime it's hot and at night it's cold, but hey I have a bed.

One of the first things I did was try to call home but my cell phone had no signal. Roxane called Verizon and asked if they provided service in Afghanistan and they said yes. They lied, unless there is an Afghanistan, Texas. If there is an Afghanistan, Texas, I'm going to have to find someone that lives there so I can call them since I'm apparently paying for it.

I don't know how much international service is going to cost me, but I'm sure my wife will have it straightened out. I just can't get over Verizon saying they had service here. I also can't get over the fact I even asked, knowing the whole country's infrastructure has already been destroyed.

Roxane will get it fixed, I have no doubt. She is very good at that sort of thing. In her mind if we owe a bill it gets paid, but if we don't . . . She scares me, and I feel sorry for whoever is trying to mess with her checkbook.

I am not allowed to talk to bill collectors anymore. My wife says I just don't have the talent it takes to communicate with other people in a manner that would leave all parties feeling like they won the battle.

With me she says I agree to pay anybody that claims I owe a bill or throw a monkey wrench into the fray that is going to get us sued over a legitimate $10 charge.

When she made up this new rule, banning me from talking to bill collectors, it was really over nothing.

Before cell phones were popular, our local phone company called and I answered the telephone because it was ringing. The nice lady on the line started explaining to me that I was behind on my monthly payments and I was just as nice but I did not have the same opinion.

Well let me tell you, this nice lady turned evil very quickly and threatened to have my phone service terminated. I let her know real quick that I'm not interested in a lecture from a woman who will more than likely run out from under the porch to bite the mailman, and that if she was going to have my phone service cut off then just do it, and I hung up on her.

After my wife spent the next two hours at one of the neighbor's houses (she had to go use their phone, ours seemed not to be working properly), she returned, very unhappy.

She explained to me, in a tone that reminded me

of the bill collector, that it had been a mistake on the phone company's part because she had already made the payment. She continued, in that same tone I might add, that she would be the only one talking to any collection agency from that moment on.

I let the tone in her voice slide. She is very lucky. OK, OK, she scares me. I was messing with her checkbook. If you call my house today, I don't answer the phone.

OK, back to my story line.

I have most of Sunday off to try and get over the jet lag. We have a 5:00 p.m. meeting and then we have a few days of training here at the base.

It is funny how the time zones mess you up. The guy in the bed next to me woke up while I was writing this email thinking it was 7:30 a.m. Sunday and was in a hurry because he didn't want to miss breakfast.

I didn't know what time it was either but I thought it was Saturday night. We looked outside and could see what looked like a sunrise coming over the mountains so we got ready for breakfast.

We killed enough time gathering our toothbrush and shaving gear that the sunrise disappeared. It was in fact Saturday night and now I am back in bed finishing my letter. Right now, it is 8:30 p.m., Saturday, May 24, but back home it is 11:00 a.m., Saturday, May 24.

Yes, we both feel pretty stupid but I think it will stay a secret. If he does not tell, I won't either. Not until now anyway.

When the real dawn showed its face, I decided to go walk about. OK, pretty lame, just in case you didn't catch that, I typed "go walk about" with my Australian accent. Here it is again with a Texas accent. Let's saddle up, boys! Grub's a'waitin' on us somewheres! In plain English I just wanted to get a look at where I was located in the scheme of the camp. In other words I needed to find the bathroom closest to my sleeping quarters and then a place to eat. I started out hungry when I thought it was time for breakfast but by now, I was absolutely starving.

I walked out of the monster tent into one of the most beautiful mornings I have ever seen in my life. Granted there was a faint essence of dirty socks from the tent, but it was beautiful all the same.

At this time of year, winter is quickly retreating high into the Himalayan Mountain Range. The snow has melted in the valley where the military base is located but the morning is still seriously cold, with the wind blowing straight down the mountainside.

As I stepped outside, I was squinting against the bright morning sunshine and walking on rocks. At first, all I thought about was how much this felt like camping in a rock quarry. No grass, no color, just that bright light blinding me and a cold wind blowing dust into my face.

This day was already starting out bad. Then as my eyes adjusted, I was able to look up.

It was breathtaking. I was standing outside an army tent in the middle of a mile-high desert at the base of a mountain range rising thousands of feet above our camp.

The snow is still on the mountainsides from about the halfway point to the top. The sky did not have a cloud in it but I could see the snow blowing off the tops of the mountains with such force it should have been raining on us below.

My wife and I were fortunate enough to be able to go see Niagara Falls one year, and the mist and fog that builds up at the base of the falls is the only thing I have ever seen that can compare with this mountain view.

It truly was a glorious sight, but I would soon learn the spring in Afghanistan brings more than just pretty scenery; it also marks the season of danger. While the snow lasts in the mountain passes, it helps keep the Taliban and insurgents out of the valley below.

The snow falls quickly as winter sets in, but it melts even faster. At the time I arrived, the nights in camp got down to below freezing, but the temperature soared to over one hundred degrees by 9:00 a.m.

I was issued a sleeping bag the night I arrived but had to go to the post exchange to buy a pillow. I could not find a sheet to buy so I bought a rug to use as a blanket.

In this heat the sleeping bag is too hot and I wanted something lighter. I seriously considered buying a ladies dress to use as a sheet. A tent with fifty guys was the deciding factor for my decision to purchase the rug.

I am done for now, but I am sure as things develop I will have more interesting news about how I spend my days here.

Charles

12

bathroom, head, latrine

As a child, I was taught the proper terminology to use when I needed to relieve myself. I grew up hearing the calls of, "Run to the bathroom! Run!" Or, "Do you need to use the toilet? If you do, you had better go now because we are not stopping."

I even had occasion to use an outhouse several times when visiting family members in Woden, Texas. I still remember the stink and having to sit in that wooden box that seemed to stay wet no matter how hot and dry the weather was, along with the bright little green flies that liked to hang out in it.

And as frequently as not I might hear, "Run behind that tree, nobody can see you." Or I heard this one most often: "If you want to know where the restroom is, just ask Charles. No matter where we go, that's the first place he has to run to." Even today, how many kids do you know who don't need to go at the most inopportune or embarrassing moments?

I enlisted in the US Army at age sixteen and still wet behind the ears. My butt cheeks still had that moist feeling from the last visit to the outhouse ten years earlier.

I learned in a very polite manner from a fellow wearing a Smoky Bear hat that all the things I had learned from Mom and Dad were hogwash. As a matter of fact, I learned that I didn't have a mama or daddy unless Uncle Sam issued them to me. I learned that my mind was mush and I was now going to have to learn everything all over again starting with the proper way to complete a push-up.

I did not realize my parents had failed so badly in teaching me these things the right way to begin with. According to the army, I was dumb as a rock. Can you believe, I didn't even know the proper terminology to express my desire to go and relieve myself until the army taught me?

It's called a latrine! If I forgot that, the proper term was latrine! This nice man in the hat would help me try and remember. He would even stand there and practice saying the word over and over again all the while I was learning the squat & thrust or the new and improved ways of doing push-ups.

Sometimes he would even get so enthusiastic about helping me remember stuff, he would ask that everyone in my company join in. Those were the times that helped me the most. I never understood why the rest of the guys didn't seem to like me as much as . . . what was he called again . . . oh yeah, the drill sergeant.

I was in the army now and finally out of boot camp. The drill sergeant even said I had graduated from being a maggot.

It wasn't too long after that when the US Marine barracks in Beirut, Lebanon, were attacked, killing 241 American servicemen and injuring 60 more. A group calling themselves Islamic Jihad claimed to have carried out the suicide bombing attacks with the backing of the Islamic Republic of Iran.

It sounds a lot like the same folks who are still trying to kill us today.

My company, Delta 4-4, was called up along with many others expecting to be going to war. I still remember the anger and eagerness we all felt. It was a righteous anger and an eagerness to defend America. I don't remember anyone being scared. That same American ire flows through our troops today. God bless them all.

To this day I don't understand why we were given the stand down order, but because of that decision I was spared the tragedy of combat firsthand. What I will be experiencing here are the same emotions our troops are feeling now and I will do my best to bring them water, fuel, or anything else that I can haul in a truck that will make their lives a little better.

I don't know how I got so sidetracked when my intent was to help educate you, the reader, on what a potty is.

While I was in the barracks at Ft. Leonard Wood, Missouri, the latrine was a modern facility with ceramic tile and porcelain sinks and showers. Unfortunately, there was some strange fetish with what is known as bivouacking.

That is where we would have to go set up camp far away from electricity and running water. Each time my platoon was pulled out into the countryside to bivouac, we were told to expect a two-to-four week stay.

Each time a squad would pull latrine duty. This consisted of digging a ditch about ten feet long and three feet deep. We would crisscross some stakes and drive them in the ground, fastening them to each other so they would have a V shape at the top about knee high. This V shape would then hold another log creating a seat over the new ditch.

I think you get the picture. That is a latrine!

If we were to stay anywhere close to a month, it would have required incinerating the contents of the latrine every now and again.

As it turned out almost all the time, we would pack up and go back to base depending on the wind. Simple thing—as long as the wind was in our favor, we stayed; but as soon as we found ourselves on the backside of that ditch, we took off.

Now moving along . . . when my company was called up to ready itself to go to war, it caused me grief even though we never left the base.

It turned out that I would not have been allowed to go anyway. You have to be eighteen years old before the army will ship you overseas.

A few months after the Lebanese bombing of the US Marine barracks, I received orders sending me to

Guam. And that is when I found out I couldn't go. Every one of my friends left and I had to stay behind because I was still wet behind the ears.

An officer called me out of ranks to verify my age, hoping it was not true. I was seventeen years old by this time but still not allowed to go with the rest of my platoon. As a matter of fact, I came real close to being sent home because I was in limbo and had no job assignment.

A few weeks later, this same officer approached and gave me my options. I could be transferred to a US Army Reserve command in Texas until I turned eighteen or take up an offer from the US Coast Guard in an Inter-Service Transfer.

The best decision of my life, besides my wife and kids, was when I joined the US Coast Guard. But guess what?

They don't even know what a latrine is! I just found out I'm as dumb as sea sponge.

Hey, sailor, what are you holding yourself so funny for? You need somebody to hold your hand and show you what a head is used for? Latrine! Drop and give me twenty, sailor. I can see we gonna have to train you all over again, your mind is nothing but seaweed. You will need to be learning how to do a proper push-up too.

Man, to think I ran away from home at sixteen because I was tired of being told what to do. I was one of those smart kids who knew everything, and I joined the service so I could be my own man! Tired of people bossing me around. I'll show them. Yeah . . . I can tell them what the difference is between a bathroom, a latrine, and a head . . . nothing!

Now I want to describe what it is like over here when you find yourself with need to relieve yourself!

For our most basic needs, there is the good old Johnny on the spot. Thousands of Johnnies on the spot I should say. Everyone will most likely know what these look like, but I will offer a brief description anyway.

At night or early in the morning the Johnny on the spot is a man-sized plastic box with a door. Inside you find the urinal molded into the side of the wall and a toilet on the back wall. It will be cool and sometimes cold and in most cases for the blue cans the odor is not so bad and they are kept clean by contract workers on a daily basis.

In the afternoon things change drastically. These little blue boxes become unbearable. They are no longer houses of retreat and relief but sweatboxes. With the sun beating down on them at 125 degrees, the plastic wants to flow in liquid form, almost. You know it is going to be miserable when you just have to go and the blue box is wilting in the sun.

Now step into one. Oooohh my God! Hot is not the word for it. No matter how clean it is, the heat still boils the stink up. I learned real quick these boxes are a last resort just to go take a leak and God forbid anyone has an upset stomach because a person could die of dehydration before any relief came to them.

You're probably wondering why I keep emphasizing the color of the Johnny on the spots. Well, this is why.

The contractors and soldiers can use any porta-potty they want, but the local Afghan workers can only use the gray ones.

Using two different colors for different people sounds like segregation, but you will understand in a moment.. Close your eyes and just pretend this is what you have to look forward to the next time the Gotta-Go Monster is dragging you off in a desperate hurry and you have to choose the closer gray box or the blue box that is just a bit further down the trail.

The local villages that supply workers to the base have very different bathrooms habits than what I am used to and most likely different than anyone reading this.

I am sure most people have seen videos or photos of the people over here and in many of those images, the local people will be squatting on their heels with their knees pointed outward. For me this position is very uncomfortable because the muscles in my legs and hips just do not like to be cramped like that. My bottom has been trained from birth to sit in a chair or sit on the ground and lean against something.

Our Afghan helpers also use the bathroom in this position. Try to imagine a person who has never seen a toilet before. This person is told for sanitary reasons he has to use a plastic box like everyone else, no more leaving it behind a building or truck or beside the road.

He walks into this box, climbs up onto the seat, and squats over the hole. He is not sitting on it but over it.

Now the Gotta-Go Monster drags you to the same one the local person just came out of or maybe a dozen before him, and look at what you find. An empty water bottle, muddy shoe prints on top of the toilet seat, and guess what? His aim was a bit off. With the diet the Afghan people have, there is not much solidity to what you see dripping over the edge of the toilet seat.

Is it easier to educate a people to conform to your habits or just supply them with their very own gray box? Segregation or smart?

Remember the empty water bottle? Our local help do not use toilet paper. I do not know why but the water in the hand with a little splashing and rubbing and rinsing are their preferred method. Thus, the invention of fist bumping came to Afghanistan with me.

Every time I see someone squatting beside the road with a smile and a wave I will be wondering if he is just sitting there waiting for something or if he is about to stand up and start kicking sand over his very own creation.

I told you about the basics now to something unique.

Shipping containers can be used for much more than shipping and storage.

What each village has in addition to the portable toilet is the shipping container toilet. We have several in our compound.

Take two rows of shipping containers with one row on top of the other. The things are designed to lock together like LEGOs so they are not going to fall apart especially after they have been welded together.

The bottom row has been converted into water-holding tanks by simply welding metal plates inside and then adding a pump and water heater.

The top row has been converted into bathrooms and showers.

From the outside, they look like a dozen shipping containers stacked together on a cargo ship, but on the inside it looks like a gymnasium locker room. It is pretty cool.

13

our village

There are many different contract companies here in Afghanistan besides the one I work for. Not all are as prestigious and most still find themselves subcontracted for my company. Nevertheless, we all live in the same type of housing.

Each company has their own compound fenced off to keep a somewhat controlled environment. The companies working over here come from all over the world, not just the United States. It is like a little piece of diplomatic soil, I guess.

As we work around the base, we all cross paths at some point, but at the end of the day everyone goes home to their own little village. Each village takes on a lifestyle depicting the origins of its countries' contract workers.

The village I live in obviously is mostly American. No matter how many people I see and talk to from different parts of the world while working, it is good to be able to come home to something familiar. I may still be in a foreign country, but our village is a little piece of America.

We have many tents like the one I described earlier; we have B-Huts and Sea-Cans to live in.

The big tents are for temporary housing and of course smell like mildewed canvas, but it's not long before you get moved up to middle class and get to live in a B-Hut.

B-Huts are built out of plywood and two-by-fours. They are not much to look at but after having to sleep in the tents a B-Hut makes you feel like you have been accepted from a homeless shelter into the community. You actually live in a little house. Sure, you have seven other guys sharing the same sixteen-by thirty-two-foot building, but it's not a tent.

The B-Hut can be modified by the occupants, such as putting up walls and doors or building shelves and beds. Some of these B-Huts should be featured in a modern home-building magazine on how to create the Ultimate Man Cave in a 6' x 8' space using scraps of lumber scavenged from wooden pallets and crates.

My B-Hut was not much to look at when I first moved in. I guess the guy who lived in it before me was just lazy or had no imagination. I had a bed with a board nailed to the wall in order to use it as a shelf. I also had a shelf that was about to fall down on the opposite side of the room.

My friends King Richard, Robbin, Bennie, and Curtis all brought me gifts. Can you get that image in your head? Yes, these men brought me house-warming gifts, so to speak, and helped me make my B-Hut livable or at least more comfortable.

I can't leave out my bosses Ed and René because by the end of my first day all of these guys would make sure I had shelves installed, a nightstand with a lamp, and a door that I could lock behind me when I left.

King Richard had friends in one of the army camps and they gave him a big metal filing cabinet that was a luxury for sure to keep my clothes in like a dresser. Most people had to use big plastic storage boxes you could purchase from the PX.

Let me describe a few of these crate-homes-away-from-home B-Huts.

Robbin: The neatest, cleanest place in the entire village. The dust and sand blowing around in Bagram can get into everything and everywhere except Robbins room. Keep in mind all of the rooms are only six feet by eight feet. When you open the door, he has a homemade bed frame that takes up the entire left side of the room.

The bed's headboard is built into the front wall with shelves and a television shelf at the foot. There is a refrigerator and boxes of microwave snacks. Lights in just the right places to throw a glow in every corner. Robbin even has a computer shelf. There is plastic around the top and corners of his room to try to keep the dust out.

Do not ask me where the refrigerator came from because I don't know.

King Richard: The closest friend I made while in

Bagram was like a bear going into hibernation when he entered his B-Hut. When walking into his room it is nothing but wall-to-wall shelves and a set of bunk beds. Knowing the King, he probably had a full-sized desk and refrigerator.

The shelves were full, the unused bunk stacked to the top and now as I am describing it I do remember him having a desk because he kept a computer on it. He has a handmade smoking jacket and tailored suits that would cost thousands of dollars in the States, so he is not just collecting junk.

The entire room was packed from floor to ceiling from years of collecting souvenirs from both Iraq and Afghanistan. Anything you can get in the United States you can get here, only about a thousand times cheaper, and King Richard had at least one of everything. The King is a large man and with all of his collection, he fits snugly like a bear in a cave. I believe he can sit at his computer and have everything a man could want to eat, drink, or play with at a hand's reach.

I would have to call King Richard the Corporal Klinger of KBR Village because if you needed it or wanted it, the King could get it.

Bennie: Big man, and I mean big, ex-pro-football-player big. Bennie figured out how to make such a small space work for him.

Instead of building the conventional room and then trying to fit himself and his belongings into it, Bennie built the room around himself. I always enjoyed visiting him because I was in awe of his living quarters.

Bennie raised his bunk up to the roof with just enough room to get in and sleep. He used the space under the bed to build a full-sized office desk with his computer and Xbox game on top of it. He also had shelves covering the walls and everything had its place.

I can't describe Bennie's room as being neat and tidy, but that's only because, like so many others, he has accumulated so much stuff that it just cannot be neat.

Curtis: I don't know what the word is I'm looking for to describe the room Curtis created inside his B-Hut. Curtis has been here long enough to carve himself out quite a little suite. He had a friend living in the room next to his that ended up going back home.

Before anyone moved into the room, Curtis knocked the wall down and extended his empire to claim both rooms. It may sound like he is being selfish but it's not that way at all, because the wall can go back up just as easily as it came down. The thing is, nobody wants to intrude on such a spectacular Pimp Den.

Walking into the room created by Curtis is more like walking into a backroom at a blues club. It has soft lighting in just the places you need it with the rest of the room mostly dark and cool. I half expect to find velvet drapes, fuzzy dice, and incense burning . . . but that is just my impression.

Curtis is a John Deer Tractor nut and his room is decorated with anything from John Deer. If John Deer sold fuzzy dice, they would be in this room.

There is music playing all the time, ("I'm too Sexy for My Tractor") in the background. Cabinets line the front wall above a couch. Yes, a big stuffed couch facing a wide-screen television that is sitting on top of a full-sized chest of drawers.

A computer sits on another desk and a second television is in a cabinet at the foot of his bed. The bed itself is about waist high with drawers that slide out to make up the frame. A second bunk is made up at the other end of the suite for guests and a guitar is propped up in the corner for proper entertainment.

These are just a few of the many people creating a little place they can call home at the end of the day, something that has a door on it and the world outside can be shut out for just a little while.

Each room in a B-Hut can be wired for television and Internet . . . for a price, of course, but I will get into that in another chapter.

There is an air conditioner mounted above each door at separate ends of the building. I forgot to mention that the B-Hut is separated down the center by a narrow hall with four rooms on each side. You can completely close off your room from top to bottom, but you sacrifice the air-conditioning.

I have described the bathrooms, fifty-man tents, and now the B-Huts, but let us go on to the best.

Sea-Can: I cannot give a personal account of what these quarters are like, but I will try my best to describe them.

Remember how I described the shipping-container bathrooms? Well, these are the same things. These containers are stacked four to six high and three wide. An outside stairway takes you to whatever level you live. The Sea-Can is just like the B-Hut only fire resistant and made of metal, so they are stronger and can accommodate more people.

The Sea-Cans are constructed very quickly. In just a few days, these things can be put into service with rows upon rows that look like apartments.

Now take all the different housing arrangements and imagine a thousand separate buildings with only six feet between them. It is easy to become lost in the maze.

14

dining facility, aka DIFAC

The most important facility on the base as far as I am concerned is the one that forks over the groceries.

While I was in Houston, we were told to expect to eat a lot of MREs. These are Meals Ready to Eat. They have come a long way from the old C-rations and K-rations that were packed into cans.

The MRE is packaged into a very sturdy and compact plastic. With the C-ration you at least had a John Wayne, aka P-38 . . . a thumb-print-sized can opener you could attach to your dog tags. Not so with the MRE.

Some of these things are so tough, a man could starve to death trying to tear into one.

I have had the privilege to dine on both types of pre-packaged meals and to tell the truth I preferred the C-rations when it came to taste.

The MRE does have improvements though, such as having a heating pad packaged with the meal so there is no need to start a fire to heat it up. It is very simple—place your plastic bag of food inside the heating bag and add water. Something in the heating bag reacts with the water and heats up instantly, giving you a little oven.

The meals can be eaten without being heated, but at least you have the option.

Anyway, I arrived in Afghanistan expecting to be living on these things but guess what, I have never eaten better in my life.

I know our troops in the field will be living on rations, but when they come back to the base they are being treated to the finest dining Afghanistan has ever known.

There are several DIFACs on the base and I eat at the one I am nearest to when it is mealtime.

All of them are similar in structure and meal choices. With such a diverse group of people to feed, there are choices at mealtimes to satisfy any person no matter what country they come from.

When it is time to eat you go to whatever DIFAC you want and swipe your meal card. Of course, the military is always on duty so you face heavy scrutiny as well as the card swipe.

There are steam tables with every kind of vegetable and meat you can think of and salad bars, fruit bars with fresh fruit, desert bars, and even someone serving up ice cream with all the fixins just like Baskin Robbins.

One of the ways you know the Taliban have hit a convoy is when there is no fresh fruit. Things like that may be reported over the news back home before we learn about it here, but there are still telltale signs that we can all guess at.

A good way to get the picture in your head of what a DIFAC looks like is by comparing it to a Wyatt's or Lubys, supersized.

15

can you trust your friends?

All of the meals are prepared by contract workers and the cleaning staff may consist of some local Afghan people. For good reason, the local help are not allowed to help with food preparation.

This is a good time to explain why. Although the airbase is the stronghold for our forces in Afghanistan, the Taliban still sneak into the villages just outside the fences, thereby controlling them with fear tactics.

Any local Afghan helper is subject to blackmail and may have no choice but to try and harm anyone they can inside the base. This being said, friendships with our helpers are guarded at all times and if it appears that a contractor and Afghan helper are becoming too chummy they are likely to be separated.

The Afghan people are not our enemy, the Taliban are. My two favorite helpers are Popal and Broder (whom I will talk about later), and they are very good people and my friends.

The part I have to remind myself of is the fact that either one of these guys may be my friend one day and the next day the Taliban may be threatening their family. The Taliban may threaten to kill their family unless one of my friendly helpers does something to harm me or someone else. Every day our helpers are being watched and if anything seems a bit off in their habits or attitude, it is up to me to notice it.

It is sad that such good people are governed by fear and because of that fear, they cannot be trusted as true friends.

16

post exchange, aka PX

Anybody and everybody knows what a PX is, or they should anyway. The PX or post exchange is the local general store on the base.

It is like a very small Wal-Mart and a Mom & Pop Farmers Mercantile all rolled into one. The PX buys supplies in bulk to save money just like Wal-Mart, but if you need something they do not have, all you have to do is ask and it can be special ordered like a Mom & Pop.

This PX is not a large one, but a lot of merchandise flows through it every day. Everyone shops here, both the military and the contractors.

The PX stays packed with people all the time and they all want the same thing I want and they usually beat me to it. You can buy snacks, clothes, boots, and computers tax-free.

I tried to stay out of the PX unless I just had to go.

Fighting the crowd for thirty minutes only to find the shelf empty is not something I enjoy. When I needed something that was not there I would ask the person in charge of the store when I could expect it on the shelf and try to be there as early as possible on that day.

The post exchange is the heart of any base and it is no different here. The PX can boost morale simply by having its doors open so a soldier can browse and lose himself down some aisle that is interesting to him or her.

In this place, the PX may be the heart but it is only the center of a larger shopping complex. It is almost like going to the city for a day of shopping.

17

city inside

Where am I? I ask myself as I stand among a milling crowd of shoppers. I am in the desert, high in the valleys of Afghanistan, and I find myself dodging shoppers as if I were in a mall doing some last-minute Christmas shopping. Wow!

The PX is not the only thing keeping up morale here. Check this out, a Dairy Queen mobile restaurant. An 18-wheeler trailer has been converted for Dairy Queen to cook and serve everything from the Hunger-Buster and fries to a Blizzard. One thing I noticed is the ice cream just does not stay frozen. Even if they serve it to you in a somewhat solid form in this heat, you only have seconds to eat it before it melts.

Under a covered pavilion is a Pizza Joint and Taco Bell.

A Green Bean coffee house is next to the PX for a cup of hot java or an exotic coffee drink of your choice.

The story I have been told is that Starbucks refused to support the war effort so they were ousted and The Green Bean is now the coffee house of choice by the military. Like I said, that is hearsay but I can say for certain The Green Bean is in Bagram.

Burger King is in Bagram! I get a kick out of watching some of the soldiers when they order fifteen or twenty burgers to go and I know they do not intend to share, but intend to eat every burger they bought.

There is a cell phone provider here and another company to provide Internet and satellite TV services.

Want jewelry? A jewelry store is just around the corner along with a store that sells fabric for custom rugs.

I never expected this kind of service in the desert, but it is an important morale booster for sure.

18

there is a hole in the roof

I have been here for two nights now, this being my second night.

I do not have much to say tonight. It is Sunday and we start our orientation in the morning. Tuesday is when we all find out where our permanent assignment will be. I hope to stay here on the base, but I won't know till Tuesday.

I already told you about the tent we are staying in, but around 12:30 a.m., I discovered something else interesting about it. There is a hole in the roof. Can you guess where this particular hole was located? Yep . . . Right above the middle of my chest. Hehe, you thought I meant my forehead..

My first thought was to try and sleep through it. My second thought was to put a Breathe Right nose strip over the hole. That lasted until I fell asleep and it started to drip again.

You have to understand why I really hated to go for my third option, and that was to move my bunk. I am at the very end of the tent and the only way I could get out of this water torture was to move closer to the guy in the next bunk. This fellow is nice to talk to in the daylight but he might not be so nice if he woke up and found me sliding over toward him in the dark, or worse maybe he would even be nicer.

Fortunately for me, he was awake and could see me trying to block the water with my nose strip and he moved his bunk enough so we could sleep in our own space. I told you he was a nice guy. We woke this morning still men and able to look each other in the eye.

The base here is surrounded by mountains, some of them still snowcapped. It is strange that in the heat of the day you can't see them for the dust in the air but after the rain last night the air was cleared. It really is a beautiful sight. I wish I could take pictures but that is prohibited by the guys toting the guns around here. They say no pictures; I say OK, I didn't really want a picture anyway.

I have a special friend at the top of my email list who has requested a uniquely Afghanistan souvenir. You know who you are. I dug out some real genuine Afghanistan earwax and I am going to save it for you. I will have to hide it in my suitcase because everybody will want to do it for their friends and then it won't be so unique anymore.

Oh, I really do appreciate the comments I have received; to be honest I'm a bit shocked at how many of you have written me back. I don't expect it and that makes it all the much better when you do, thanks. And no, I'm not trying to pressure anybody to write me because this is more like what another friend said, like a journal. It didn't start life that way but it is turning into an open diary, so no response is required. I will correspond on a personal basis to you as I have time though.

Talk to y'all later,
Charles

19

reality check

This morning, my first Monday morning in Afghanistan, has been a reality check for me.

Since I have been here, I have not felt threatened at all because there is a large military presence at this base. But this morning while walking from the DIFAC (dining facility) we were directed to stand on the shoulder of the roadway by an MP. I had no idea what was happening but soldiers and contractors alike were just lined up and down both sides of the roadway.

The small group I was standing with started making jokes about what was happening with me being right in the middle. We were enjoying this thing that was happening because we didn't know why we had to stand there. We were making jokes about how the military is trained that if you see a line, then get in it.

I could see an MP vehicle with blue lights flashing escorting another military vehicle. I was thinking it might be the base commander when I saw all the soldiers salute one by one as the vehicle passed by. Then right before they got to me, I realized the contractor personnel were removing their headgear.

The military escort passed by as I removed my hat. I finally realized what was happening, and my joking mood shifted to a very somber one that I have not been able to shake yet.

The second vehicle was a military Hummer with a US-flag-draped casket sitting in the back.

One of our soldiers was killed last night. I don't know how or where but it didn't matter. It brought about the realization that this base is not the whole of the war effort in Afghanistan. I have always held our servicemen in high regard, but this has changed my attitude even more toward the grateful end of the spectrum.

I have been looking at the young men in the DIFAC and I remember what it was like for me when I joined the army. These guys are only seventeen to twenty years old and they are very impressive in their physical fitness and make me proud that they represent me, but they haven't even lived a life yet and they are willing to give it up for another's freedom.

I won't harp on the funeral procession anymore because we all see it on the TV and read about it in the newspaper, but this was personal and I will never forget it. The most profound part was the deep feeling of respect for their fallen comrade that the soldiers expressed. I felt like an outsider looking in on a private ritual.

Today I will go to orientation and tomorrow I will find out just where I will end up. Wish me luck because I would like to stay here.

You know, all of these emails will go out at the same time. I have to write them and store them for now because I have no way to transmit them. Hopefully you won't be so overwhelmed that you decide not to read them.

Talk to you later,
Charles

20

mortar fire

Well, I experienced my first mortar fire last night. I can't say it was a mortar attack because it was too far away. But it was interesting nonetheless. After counting off nine rounds and observing that nobody nearby was getting too excited, I just went back to sleep.

In the event we are attacked, I have been issued a helmet and body armor and I have a bunker to run to. The bunkers are made of concrete and reinforced with sandbags. There are enough bunkers for the entire village to hunker down in.

I hope I will not have to experience an attack that would send me to the bunkers because the guys that have been here a while say you may have to stay in the bunker from just a few minutes to several days.

It's funny, I'm sitting here writing in my lunch hour and an announcement just came over the loudspeaker saying there was going to be a controlled detonation in the next five minutes. That means they found an unexploded mortar round or land mine and the army is going to blow it up. They tell us this so nobody will panic when the explosion takes place.

I will find out this afternoon exactly where I will be working.

Talk to you later,
Charles

21

my new job; driver-heavy truck

They got the heavy right.

I get to stay in Bagram and on base. That is an answer to prayer for me. I contracted to go wherever the military needed me and that could have been anywhere in Iraq or Afghanistan.

Afghanistan has proven to be a more dangerous place to be assigned than Iraq, but the jobs are just now shifting from Iraq to Afghanistan.

It is something to make note of if you are curious as to where a big military operation may take place in the near future. That is to watch where the contract labor is building up. Since the military relies on civilian labor so our troops can concentrate on the fighting, you will see a huge transfer of manpower and resources before the military ever arrives.

That is what is happening in Afghanistan. The military

is about to beef up their presence in Afghanistan and start withdrawing troops from Iraq at the same time.

If I had gone to Iraq, by the time I was settled in real good I would have had to pack up and ship off to Afghanistan anyway.

What I am going to be doing is driving a tank truck full of water.

The military has managed to drill several deep wells to find water and even built a water treatment plant. I do not know how deep you have to go to find water here, or I should say good water. Then again, the local villagers have wells they dug by hand and even have an irrigation system for their gardens.

The deep wells are fenced off with security and the water is pumped into giant rubber bladders that are lying on top of the ground. The trucks pull up to a big valve outside the fence and the water is then pumped into the trucks.

The water being pumped out of the ground and into the trucks is not for drinking but is used to provide showers and toilet water as well as being used for washing vehicles or aircraft, etc.

We have about fourteen small three thousand-gallon tank trucks and two ten thousand-gallon tank trucks. I don't know the actual amount of water being pumped, but considering the trucks run twenty four hours a day with the small ones loaded four to five times a day and the big ones at least twice a day, that adds up to a lot of water.

I am going to start out riding with another driver on one of the smaller trucks in order to learn a route, but I already know I will move to the larger truck soon because out of all the drivers here only a few have experience on such a large truck and trailer.

I have (too much) experience with the big, long-wheel-base, extended-hood trucks and fifty-three-foot trailers in cities such as New York and Chicago. In fact, I have driven a big rig in every state in the lower forty-eight and in every major city, so even the ten thousand-gallon tanker is small to me.

The route I am going to learn covers two dining facilities, the food court, and the wash rack. All of the stops on this route have several five hundred-gallon tanks each that I will pump water into.

One of the DIFACs has four of these tanks and they can go through that much water during lunch so I will have to fill those tanks up two or three times a day.

While I am training, I will have to hook up the hoses and be the ground guide for the driver to help him get the truck backed in to certain tight areas.

The driver is telling me how good it is to have me help him because I can speak English. He says most days are spent just pointing and grunting because his helper cannot speak enough English and he cannot speak Farsi.

The driver knows where to go and the helper knows what to do when he gets there, so talking is not needed. The helpers live in the local village just outside the fences and have been working this job longer than most of the drivers anyway. When the driver goes home, another driver replaces him, but the helpers always stay.

22

the camel spider

OK, I now have a job and have been here for two days. I drive a water tanker. I don't leave the base so all I have to worry about are mortar rounds and the occasional rocket or man-eating animals.

Yes, I said animals. I have learned that Afghanistan is such a primitive country (even before the United States bombed the Taliban back into the Stone Age) that there is no catalog of insects or animals here. I understand a British fellow wrote a book in the 1950s but he had only been in the country for three months, so it was very incomplete.

To start with, and by far the most interesting to me, is the fact that all of Afghanistan's wild animals or indigenous animals eat meat.

Back home when we think of a spider's diet we automatically think of the poor misunderstood fly, right? Well, here the spider might eat the fly but they also eat bigger things like camels. The spider I'm talking about is actually called a camel spider, and they are normally the size of your hand.

The camel spider will crawl under a sleeping camel and start eating it while it sleeps. When the camel wakes up, he has a big hole in his stomach. How gross is that?

You know what I think would be cool? I would like to see a spider web big enough to catch a camel.

They are not poisonous and I understand they are very beneficial because they eat all the mice and insects they can catch, which make the people here very happy.

This is one of those spiders that if Roxane found it hiding in the bathroom and screamed for me to kill it, I would throw her the shotgun and wish her luck.

The rabbits here even eat meat. It is not uncommon in the States for mama rabbits to eat their own young, but these rabbits over here are even bigger than Texas jackrabbits and will eat each other or a dead animal.

You have a 50-50 chance when it comes to eating an Afghanistan chicken because you have a 50 percent chance the chicken will eat you.

I will write more about the local people as I learn about them. Right now I have very mixed thoughts about them and don't want to commit my thoughts in writing until I'm certain I know what I'm telling you. I can say this culture is nothing like I have ever seen or even read about. I was not prepared to meet a people with such a different way of doing simple things like eating, bathing, and socializing. I will have a local helper assigned to my charge starting next week and

I'm sure I will learn firsthand a few interesting things to tell you about.

One more thing about the animals here before I go. My boss told me a few months ago that a local farmer had his herd of goats too close to the base and one of the goats stepped on a land mine. He said the goat's hindquarter landed on his windshield. You have to understand there were over eleven million mines buried here and most of them are still unaccounted for.

I know I have kind of rambled in this one, but I am so tired I can barely write at all. Have I ever mentioned how hot it is here? I'm going to sleep now and I will try to be more entertaining in the next email.

Charles

23

safe inside the gates

Well, this is day ten of captivity. I have only been in country for ten days and we have had four fallen comrade ceremonies. It is sad to watch.

Being here on the base you can almost forget that there is a war going on just outside. From where I live and work it almost looks like a cleanup of somebody else's mess. I mean by the anti-mining going on and all the wrecked Russian tanks and planes. In reality our troops go out into the world that exists off this base to fight the Taliban and some of them don't come back alive.

I mentioned the Russian planes and tanks. There is a graveyard here with a bunch of these in it from the time the Russians invaded Afghanistan only to be beaten back. They are neat to see and I hope to be able to get some pictures.

I have been told I will be able to take some pictures but only in certain areas, so I will have to buy a camera now.

Just outside the fence I can see a village that was destroyed by the Taliban. The entire village is made of adobe. It looks like the pictures you find in a children's Bible story.

Looking through the fence, I can see big holes blown out of the walls. I said the Taliban was responsible, but I don't know that for sure. It could have been our military that punched those holes in an effort to rout the Taliban.

Have I mentioned how hot it is?

This sun is killing me. I would say I look like a raccoon because I have a patch of skin that is covered by my sunglasses, but in reality I look like a red Indian with white war paint around my eyes. It is not a pretty sight and man I hurt. You can always tell the new guys because they walk around here blistered.

I'm sorry I haven't had any good stories to tell, but I'm just so tired by the time I get to write, all I want to do is sleep.

24

I put my foot in my mouth
. . . again

I will tell one story real quick. This happened yesterday.

I was sitting on top of a picnic table talking to my boss Ed. He came to me and said I needed to put in my request for my time to go home at the end of my four months.

My boss asked if I had a date in mind I would like and I said yes, I would like to take the time off around my wife's birthday to go home if I could.

At this point, another guy standing nearby butted into our conversation and said they don't do anniversaries, birthdays, graduations, or holidays to get people home. I politely told this man that I appreciated his comments but I wasn't talking to him and that he needed to go away.

I have been here long enough now that Ed and I have become fast friends. Ed lives just a few miles from me in Texas and he was very glad and made me feel welcome when I arrived. I have been here just long enough for him to expect me to buck up to any challenge, and in this case, when I saw his face cringe, I figured I bucked up at the wrong time.

This other guy, Kirk, turned out to be the boss of my boss, and needless to say I didn't get my wife's birthday off. I now have a date of September 25 to come home. The guys have been ribbing me for two days now because of it.

Kirk is a good fellow, too, and a lot of fun to cut up with, but now I know who the boss is.

Ed just laughed and said later how good it is to have someone to take the heat off him for a change.

I can always claim sunstroke. One look at this burnt melon of a head and you would understand why I wasn't in my right mind to tell the boss to butt out.

Charles

25

the polish soldier

Did anybody know that Poland had an army? I met them today. All five of them.

My coworker and I were sitting down to lunch when a Polish army guy sat down with us. We were friendly enough to strike up a conversation with him but of course he was hard to understand because of his thick accent. Even so, I didn't say anything about it because I was impressed he could speak English at all.

During our visit he asked why I was so sunburned. I told him I was new in country and had only been here for two weeks so the sun was really getting to me. He said he just got in and was dreading the heat and the sunburn.

I told him to look at my friend Larrel. I said Larrel had been here for two months and he started out as white as me (Larrel is a black man). The Polish guy had to look twice at Larrel before he figured out I was joking with him. The look on his face was priceless.

The Polish soldier asked me if I was from the United States and when I said yes he asked which state I was from. I of course told him Texas. He got excited to meet someone from Texas and the first thing he asked was if it was true that everybody had a gun on their hip like John Wayne. He said it is a widely known rumor in Poland that Texas is a wild country where cowboys roam the streets with pistols on their belt.

I of course cleared this little rumor up for him by saying that yes, everybody has a gun in Texas and that a six-shooter is a common gift for a two-year-old's birthday. This guy was too easy.

I finally told him I was kidding and we had a good laugh. I thought since I had a little fun at this man's expense I would leave him to finish his meal in peace so I started to get up.

This Polish guy had the nerve to tell me I couldn't speak English very well. He said it was hard for him to understand me because I had an accent. I guess you would have to be there but to have this man tell me in his own broken English that I couldn't speak English was too funny.

I say in the end he got the bigger laugh at my expense. I stabbed him with my fork and I am now writing this from the MP's office. Not really.

One little update, I was complaining about not being able to breathe when I first got here. It turns out I was having a reaction caused by the malaria medication I was required to take.

The medics told me to stop taking it, and the next morning I was back to normal. I still have gripes and complaints, but I can't blame it on the drugs anymore.

Charles

26

the war: it's real

We had another fallen comrade service today. At this rate there has been one every other day since I have been here. I'm telling you, it is the saddest thing to watch. The soldiers all come out and salute their comrade as he is taken to the plane, and all the contractors stand alongside them with their hats in their hand or over their heart.

I don't like writing about it because it puts me in a bad mood. I don't like funerals and I have a strange way of dealing with my own pain when it comes to the death of a loved one. I just cannot tell you about it because it is part of what I'm doing right now.

I'm here and I see firsthand what I have seen on the news, but now it is real. Somehow I had been able to watch the news on the war and simply dismiss it because I wasn't in it. I'm still not in the war, but when a young person is sent down that road to the plane that takes them home for the last time, and I'm here to see it, now it seems real.

Like I said before, here on the base it is easy to forget there is a war going on. Here the living conditions are rough, but aside from that it is normal. It is like any big refinery or construction site you may have seen. The only difference is you eat and sleep at work.

There are ninety different countries represented here by their military, and it is very confusing when you have that many uniforms roaming around. English is the main language spoken, but that doesn't mean you can understand it with all the thick accents.

27

my own truck

I was turned loose on my own today with my own truck and helper. My truck has two bullet holes in the cab as a reminder in case I forget where I am. I deliver water to the DIFAC and the food court next to the PX or store.

I can't say this is the easiest job I have ever had, but it sure rates right at the top. As far as a driving job, this is the easiest.

The base speed limit is 15 mph, so I only use two gears and most of the time the truck just idles to where I need to be. I have a local fellow as a helper and he does all the work. He hooks up the hoses and he stops traffic and has to walk behind the truck when I have to back up. I don't even have to fuel my own truck because they have people to do that for me.

I'm not trying to romance anybody by telling you how good it is because I still want to go home to

Mama. This is a good place to work at any trade if you can stand the heat and the living conditions. I can tell you they pay a lot of money for very little work.

Somebody needs to come over here with me to keep me company. I have been trying to get my friends Ted, Larry, and Big Mac to come drive, but they won't come. Any craft you do at home, they do it here, so come on.

Charles

28

my afghani helpers

I wasn't going to write so soon after my last email because I think a few of you are getting bored with me, but I'm going to tell you about my local Afghani helper while I'm thinking about it.

Oh yeah, I am apologizing now for those of you who are sensitive to the misspelled words and my lack of proper grammar. I can barely speak the English language (according to the Polish) and I have a meticulous buddy (John Allison) of mine to point out all my misspelled words. I have my own hang-ups but spelling isn't one of them, so to make an effort to avoid anybody else crying over my spelling you may need to stop reading so you don't hurt yourself.

John has been trying to smarten me up since we were shipmates together on the USCGC Yocona based out of Kodiak, Alaska, in the early eighties.

Back to my story.

Mohebulla is my helper's name in the morning—I have him for the first eight hours—and Amin Ghag is my helper in the afternoon—I have him for the last four hours. Both men are from the local villages.

Mohebulla speaks a language called Dari, and Amin Ghag speaks Farsi. Many of the words mean the same thing but many do not and it is confusing. When I try to communicate with them as I learn some of one language, I inevitably use it on the wrong helper.

Mohebulla says he is twenty-four years old because that is what his government ID badge says.

It is the same birthday I have seen so many times as a cop working with people from this region of the world. It simply says they were born on January 1 of whatever year they think they were born. Mohebulla is at least forty years old. He has to be, unless the desert is really that harsh on the body.

One of the things I find interesting is that their women have no names, No given name, anyway. We were talking and he asked if my wife had a name. I said her name was Roxane and he thought it was a very nice name. I in turn asked about his family and he said his wife had no name. I thought he might have been kidding me, but he was serious. His wife was a female and as such was not given a name. The women in this culture are for childbearing and working to raise the children and are not important enough to name—according to him, anyway.

Mohebulla lives in a mud or adobe house with fourteen people. They have no electricity and no running water. He has a brother who works in Kabul for $2 a day, and Mohebulla is working with me for $10 a day. That sounds like slave labor, but in this economy it is three times his average pay.

When I sit back and look at it, it seems a lot like the States. We have people coming through the fence to work for low wages and then they go home with more money than they have ever seen before. And why do they come? Because we pay them to do the things we won't do ourselves.

I'm glad to have both of these guys to help, but it is still hard to believe all they get is $10 a day. I should clarify that—they get $500 Afghani dollars a day, which equals $10 US dollars.

What I find most interesting is the way the locals interact with one another. They have a complex set of hand gestures to communicate while at a distance. My helper will be in the truck, he will make some hand gestures to someone working at the dining facility, and next thing you know that person slips my helper an apple like two kids trying to hide a note from the teacher. They communicate in a manner that you find in a prison where the inmates are not allowed to talk to one another. They find ways to communicate anyway. That's all for now,

Charles

29
land mines

Someone stepped on a land mine today. I have no way of knowing if it was a soldier, a contractor, or a local villager. I also don't know if they lived.

There were eleven million mines planted in this area by the Russians when they were fighting the Taliban. From what they told us in our orientation, 95 percent of all the mines found are by the local population. That means even though the military is actively seeking out and destroying mines every day, they have only found about 5 percent. The rest have been found by someone other than the military, either by spotting them or by stepping on them.

These mines have been here a long time and this is what happens: as the ground freezes in the winter the earth that the mines are buried in contracts, and as it warms up the same earth starts to expand, causing the mines to eventually work their way to the surface—kind of like a splinter does when you leave it alone.

We have two local villagers working with us who have had one of their feet blown off. Some of these mines will just maim you and some are powerful enough to kill you and anybody near you.

Some of these mines are still inside the fence with us, but any areas that have not been cleared by the military have been fenced off with signs warning us to stay out.

If for some reason you find yourself off the roadway that has been cleared and in an area that has not been de-mined, it could be a long wait because then the military will have to clear a path to reach you.

There is a big plane at the end of the runway that was not able to stop in time and ended up in an area with mines, so it is still there waiting to be recovered.

Where I work is right at the end of the runway and everybody heard the engines getting louder instead of dying down like they should have, and we all turned just in time to see the plane kicking up a dust storm as it ran off the pavement. Quite interesting.

The military has big bulldozer-like machines that have a huge drum with chains all around it instead of a blade. This drum spins at a high rate of speed, slapping the chains on the ground like a giant weed-eater that detonates a mine as the chains beat on them, and it just keeps going without even stopping.

There are civilian contractors here from another country who go out every day looking for mines to disarm by hand. Crazy!

Yesterday the military found a mine and called over the loudspeakers, letting us know there was going to be a controlled detonation. They tell us this so we don't think we're being bombed.

This particular mine was booby-trapped, and when they detonated it there was a second, more powerful, explosion that caused a fire near the fuel dump. It was an exciting time for the drivers called in to bring water. I wasn't one of them, but I could hear the commotion over my radio. Having a fire near a fuel dump is not the way you want to start your day.

When I left to come over here, I went to Wal-Mart and bought some new boots. These boots made my feet stink. So I went to the PX and bought some high-dollar desert tactical army boots. I like the boots, but you know what? My feet still stink.

I don't think it is the boots making my feet smell so bad; I have narrowed it down to defective socks. I know not to buy this brand anymore if they are going to smell like this.

Charles

30

attacked!

Last night was interesting. I heard a lot of gunfire and I mean it sounded like some big guns, like 50-caliber big. I knew something was happening but after about ten minutes of this, it got quiet again.

I didn't know till this morning that we had been attacked. Of course, I knew something was going on but I wasn't sure what it was.

Every now and then I will hear what sounds like a gun battle . . . but never so as close as this one.

The Taliban evidently have been working a long time trying to dig a tunnel under the fence or they found an old one in existence. A group of the enemy made their way into the camp somehow, but they chose the wrong place to sneak in.

I understand they snuck into an area where groups of army special forces were located, and it didn't go too well for the bad guys. The rumor is that all of the enemy were killed without any losses to our troops.

That is kind of like trying to rob a donut shop while fifty cops are having a coffee break.

With me being just a civilian contractor I will never know exactly what happened, but it is a scary thing to think someone out there is that crazy.

31

the mammut

Today was no less interesting. I was to take my first day off on June 12, but it was canceled. The guy driving the Mammut (that is the biggest water truck we have) is going home for his R & R, so I was asked to take over his route.

It turns out the few people who are capable of driving it don't want to because it is too big, so the new guy got stuck with it.

The funny thing is, it holds ten thousand gallons of water and is heavy, but it is a European cab-over truck with a forty-foot tank. To me that means it is about thirty feet shorter than what I had to drive into the heart of the cities back in the States. These guys are scared of it and I feel like I'm driving a toy. It is funny.

Today while I was riding and trying to memorize the route, my driver tried to make a left turn but couldn't make it because a dump truck was blocking our path.

I got out and asked the driver to move forward a little bit so we could make the turn. The dump truck driver ran over the Mammut, tearing the driver-side mirror off. I wonder now if maybe I could have asked a little nicer.

I guess I won't be driving it anytime soon. It is hard to get parts here and if they don't have another mirror stored somewhere it may take as long as four months to get one.

I asked the boss if this meant I got my day off back and he said no. We have two Mammuts here.

Oh yeah, I had a request for a Rolex watch. You know, I can buy one from the locals here for about $30. The army says no. I can't have it and I can't mail it home. They search your mail before it is mailed and the same sign that says no Rolex watches also says I can't mail any human body parts home. In other words, don't ask me to send you a Rolex or any body parts.

Yes, body parts such as hands, ears, and noses are acceptable items to have in the world outside our fence. Wallets made out of a person's ear are some of the things I can't mail home.

Well, I have to go take a tour of the airfield so I can get my flight line badge tonight. I have to have an ID made for everything here. I have more IDs now than Maxwell Smart, James Bond, and Jason Bourn put together.

I will save the flight line for another update. I want to know more about the planes before I tell you about them.

Charles

32

attacked again!

Today is a sad day for us. I told you about the attack on our base a few days ago; well, last night the Taliban attacked another smaller base nearby.

Their initial attack was forced back by the military, but this morning about 5:00 a.m. the Taliban attacked again. This time they killed two KBR contractors, and two more are injured to the point that it was said they would be better off dead.

I have no way of knowing how many others were killed or injured. Like I said before, it is hard to even remember there is a war going on sometimes and then something terrible happens to remind you.

I consider myself blessed to have been sent to Bagram Airfield because this is where all the firepower is. I do transit the outer limits of the base and would be susceptible for target practice and I sleep in an area near the outer edge of the base, but I am not worried.

I can't describe the inner workings of the base and all the military equipment here, but I can say I feel secure with these guys here to protect us.

The base that was hit so hard is a much smaller facility than where I am. My contract says I am required to go where I am needed but I think I will just come home before I go to the smaller camps. Maybe.

When I went to lunch today I got to look up close at a Hummer that had been shot. The windshield on the driver's side had been peppered with bullets but did not break through. I can't imagine sitting behind the wheel and having six or seven bullets smacking into the windshield where my head was. Some soldier will remember that experience for the rest of his life.

Today was another long day for me. It was supposed to be my day off for the Memorial Day holiday, but it was canceled. I was given first choice for the Independence Day holiday and I chose the 18th of July. That will be my first day off since I have been here and it is still a month away.

Charles

33

wrong email

I have to tell what my wife did, even though she will want to strangle me. She is a wonderful source for good stories but I don't always feel safe in telling them. Right now I am out of reach so here goes.

I have this friend . . . and no this is not the beginning of a big lie. I do have a friend. Anyway this friend . . . John . . . wanted to know what my address was over here so he could send me a care package.

I gave this address to my wife and promptly forgot it because it was now in her capable hands. I sent her an email and asked if she would send the address to John for me. It did not occur to me that she might not know what John's email address was.

Well, she did her best by searching through my email addresses and picked the one she thought must be it. This email address actually contained the name of John in it. You know where I'm going with this already, don't you?

Well, she sends a nice note to this email address and said that this was my current address and he could send me a care package if he wanted.

The next day Curtis, one of the guys I work with here, met me before we went to work. I was sitting there talking to a couple of guys when he walked up and slapped a Pop-Tart into my chest and said, "Here is your care package your wife wanted me to give you."

As you can guess, the email intended for John in Houston actually went to Curtis in Bagram, Afghanistan.

I gave the Pop-Tart to one of our local helpers who had never seen such a critter and didn't know what to do with it. I had to open it for him and he ate it like a sandwich, both tarts at the same time.

We had a big laugh about the mix-up, but the best part was watching that old man eat a Pop-Tart for the first time in his life.

Charles

34

the fishing story

I went fishing today.

I love to fish and I try to go fishing everywhere I go just to say I did.

The water was as clear as a swimming pool and I could see the bass bedding down near a group of rotted-out trees. The trees were still standing but had no leaves to give shade. The bass were hanging around the darkest part, that being the trunk of the trees, but the sun was able to shine right down and light them up anyway. I'm talking about some lunkers here, fifteen to twenty pounds apiece.

I didn't have my normal rig I like to fish with, but I did have a good fly rod. I know you think I'm crazy trying to catch a bass that big with a fly rod and with such clear water, but I didn't know what to fish with. Most of the waters I've ever bass-fished were nowhere near this clear, and most of the time they were downright muddy. I know how to fish a muddy body of water, but this was new and wonderful being able to see what I was fishing for. The main drawback was that I couldn't get very close to them because I was standing on the bank.

I had the beautiful snowcapped Himalayas behind me with a cool breeze blowing just enough to keep me comfortable but not enough to make the water ripple, so I never lost sight of my bass.

I tied on a white fly. I had no idea what these bass like to eat, but a good habit I have is looking at what surrounds the body of water I am going to fish. If it is a muddy bank with crawfish, then I will go for dark, large bait of some sort without too many things that shine like spinner baits. If the banks are covered in grass or swampy, then I go for the lighter colors and my favorite baits for this area would be a weedless frog.

I was standing on the most beautiful sandy beach beside the clearest freshwater lake I have ever seen, with the most bass I have ever seen, not to mention the largest bass I have ever seen. I didn't know what to use as bait. I was looking around and found that the area had quite a few flying ants. These ants had big white wings and when they would fall in the water these bass would suck them under. They didn't make a loud splashing sound, just a slight slurping noise and the ant was gone.

I chose my fly to match the flying ant as closely as possible.

The very first cast I made, I saw the biggest bass I have ever seen in my life coming to investigate it along with a few smaller ones. They all just looked at my fly but didn't do anything but look at it and then swam back down to their bedding area. I cast about twenty times with the same results every time. I was desperate now, I wanted a fish, I wanted the big one, but I was willing to settle for any one of them.

I thought I would try something. Thinking it was my human smell on the bait that was turning them off, I decided to fix it. I found an old tree covered with these flying ants and caught about a dozen of them. I killed them and rubbed their little bodies all over my lure, trying to transfer as much of their odor to it as possible.

I cast this time . . . and the same thing. I saw the monster bass come to look it over and just when I thought he was going to go back down, a smaller bass headed for my ant-smelling bait. I guess he thought the smaller bass was going to get the ant so he rushed back and gobbled up my bait. I didn't know what happened, one second he was going to the bottom without taking my lure and the next second he was heading to the bottom with my lure.

He caught me by surprise and almost took my rod from me. You would think after spending years fishing in water you can't see a strike coming, I would not have been caught by surprise. My heart was pounding out of my chest, my rod was about to break, I was fighting at least a twenty-pound bass on a fly rod with a seven-pound test line. I had to finesse this monster or he would break something and I would lose him for sure.

I played this bass for about twenty minutes before he started to get tired. I was walking up and down the bank trying to keep him from getting tangled up in the stand of trees he had been bedding down in. He would rip the line off the spool and I would ease it back on. This was one of the greatest fishing moments of my life.

He finally got tired and I was able to get him up to the sandy bank where I was. I pulled him in ever so gently because at any moment he could make another run for it and if I wasn't ready when he spooked, all of my efforts would be in vain.

I eased him into the shallow water and I lay down on my stomach so I could reach him without having to wade out. He gave one last splash but I had him. I had my thumb in his mouth and I wasn't letting go. He splashed so much water in my face, I had to close my eyes. When I opened my eyes again, my boss was standing over me with an empty water cup saying, "Get back to work and if I catch you sleeping on the job again you're fired. And why do you have a thumb stuck in my tuna sandwich?"

Charles

PS: This book from beginning to end is true to my experiences and knowledge except "The Fishing Story." I love to fish and a true fisherman has a little fiction in him somewhere.

35

hot and sandy

Today is a good day to be somewhere else other than Bagram, Afghanistan. The day started off hot earlier in the day than it has been. It was 104 degrees Fahrenheit by 9:00 a.m. and it was only getting started. Some parts of Afghanistan hit 126 degrees today. I think it was about 110 here where I am.

The air conditioner in my truck does not work and with a top speed of fifteen to twenty miles per hour, the heat just stays with you. What really makes it uncomfortable is the wind blowing the dust around.

I will try to explain how it feels . . . Take a hair dryer and turn it on high. Now turn it so that it is blowing straight into your face. Next, have some talcum powder and shake it out in front of the hair dryer so that it blows into your face. This sounds like I'm making it up, but that is what it is like.

The heat, believe it or not, is bearable. There is no moisture in the air so it does not feel as hot as you would think. It is the wind blowing the dust around that makes it so hard to breathe.

I started out by saying it was a bad day to be here. Well, as the day wore on the wind picked up and by the end of my shift, the sand and dust were blowing so hard it blotted out the sun. I had to drive with my headlights on so maybe somebody would see me and not step out in front of my truck while I was creeping back to the yard.

There is no place to hide from the dust. It a fine powder and it gets into everything. Today I had sand in my nose and mouth. It felt like I was eating sandpaper all day. I just hope when it comes out, it does not feel the same way.

The heat here does register higher on the thermometer than it does back home, but it truly is a different kind of heat. I know anything over a hundred degrees is just too hot, but this is a dry heat.

In Texas at 80 degrees accompanied with the humidity, it is worse than this place at 110. It is hot but not smothering. My friend Jeff in Pennsylvania wrote and said they were having a string of days in the 90s and I promise it is more uncomfortable even in Pennsylvania than here.

The hardest part about dealing with the heat is staying hydrated. That means you have to drink a lot of water, forcing yourself to drink much more than you want to. During the morning, it is easy to drink a lot because the water is still cool enough to enjoy, but in the afternoon the water is so hot you want to gag trying to swallow it.

I have taken to letting a bottle of water sit in a mud hole at each stop I make in order to cool it off enough to drink. Since I drive a water truck, I can make my own mud hole if one does not exist.

I drink a bottle of water when I go eat breakfast and one while having our morning meeting. I make myself drink one bottle of water at every stop I make and I average fifteen to seventeen stops a day. I also drink a bottle before I go to sleep. I average between eighteen and twenty bottles of water a day, and it is still not enough.

I thought I would be sweating a lot, but you don't seem to sweat here. If you do, it is very little and it comes from sitting in a seat. The back of your legs may sweat, but as soon as you get out you are dry again. The dry heat and wind combined with the ever-present dust just keeps you dry all the time. I guess you may sweat, but it evaporates immediately.

Well, I have rambled on about the heat long enough. It is going to get hotter here in the months of July and August so I will touch on it again, I'm sure.

Charles

36

upgraded

Where to begin? I am a little out of practice with my computer being down for so long . . . what, four or five months I think? Well, that's what it seems like. Yes, I know a few of you who know me really well have already told my wife I will go crazy without a computer, and I'm sure she would agree that would be a short trip for me. That's a joke for the blondes on my email list.

I have been here for over a month now and tonight I am sleeping between clean new bed sheets for the first time. I am in hog heaven.

I described the accommodations I received when I first got here, but I have since upgraded. I'm living large compared to my fifty-man tent.

I have been moved into a B-Hut. It is a small building made of plywood. Some are eight-man B-Huts and some ten. I live in an eight-man hut. Some of the rooms have walls and doors and some have sheets or blankets strung up for privacy, and some have none of this.

I am lucky, I have a room where someone built walls and a door. My room is about six feet by eight feet. It is very small but it is mine. These rooms don't come with anything but a bed, not even a light. I was issued a sleeping bag and I already told you about the rug I bought to cover up with. Someone gave me a light when I first moved in and someone else gave me a better one yesterday, so now I have a good lamp.

It is amazing how well I sleep at night because what I have described to you does not sound very comfortable, but it really is not bad. The B-Hut has a good air conditioner and Roxane sent me a small fan. Between these luxuries and being so tired at the end of the day, I sleep soundly.

The bad thing about this kind of living arrangements is you hear everything that is going on around you. For example, my next-door neighbor right at this moment is watching something on his TV. He has headphones on so the TV does not disturb anybody else, but this guy laughs to himself when he thinks something is funny. All I hear is him next door giggling to himself and at times it gets me to laughing, too, and I have no idea what he is watching. Somebody standing outside would probably think they stumbled upon a B-Hut for loonies.

While my computer was down, I did continue to takes notes so I would have something to write about later. If I were traveling the country and visiting interesting places, it would be easy on me to keep you entertained and keep you wanting news from me, but here all I do is drive around in a big circle all day long doing the same thing over and over again. I have resorted to torturing my helper just so I can write to tell you about it. So I will tell you about it soon.

Charles

37

sharing my lunch

I met one of the local wasps today, up close and personal. As a matter of fact I shared my lunch with him.

A little history first. The truck I drive is the biggest so it takes me longer to load the truck and just as long to discharge my load. It has become clear to some of the other drivers that I am not able to take a lunch break with everyone else because of the time factor.

Yesterday my friend Robbin found me and shared his meal with me. I call him my friend because he had lobster and steak. If it had been a hamburger, he would have only ranked as an acquaintance.

While on the bus going to our jobsite, I was bragging about the meal Robbin shared with me. When I say shared I don't mean we ate out of the same plate. He had two plates, which the soldiers had given him, and he gave me one. I was telling King Richard about it.

King Richard made it his mission today to try and outdo Robbin. It's hard to top a well-seasoned steak and two lobster tails.

King Richard brought me a plate with two of the finest steaks I've ever eaten and he brought my local Afghan helper a plate with chicken off the same grill. I don't know if the steaks were really as good as they seemed, but it has been a long time since "The Cattle Company" in Beaumont, Texas.

I haven't decided what meal I enjoyed the most. I think I will brag tomorrow again while we are on the bus to see if Robbin will make it his mission to feed me again.

OK, we have this plate of chicken. I gave my helper a piece of my steak (after assuring him it was beef and not pork) and he gave me a piece of his chicken.

While I was sitting there on the ground eating this chicken, a giant wasp flew over to investigate. I had already made up my mind to write about some of the insects here because they are a bit different than the ones we have back home, but this wasp earned his own story.

Everybody knows what bumble bees, red wasps, and hornets look like. Well, this thing looks like a combination of all three. He is as large as a bumble bee with his upper body the color of a red wasp and his tail black in color with a big yellow ring. He looked like a hornet on steroids.

I have seen a bunch of the wasps around but none have ever bothered me and they always seemed to be busy looking for something. Well, I found out today they are looking for chicken fresh off the grill.

Remember how I told you that everything in Afghanistan from wild dogs to rabbits eat meat? The insects here are no exception.

This wasp wanted my chicken. I tried to shoo him off but he wouldn't go away. Finally, I just let him land on my chicken. He had great big jaws like those that you see on the giant wood ants. This wasp paid no mind to me at all. He went right to work carving out a large section of my chicken; well, I should say our chicken because we were definitely sharing this meal. I kept pulling off what I wanted of the meat and eating it, and he kept right on taking his share.

When the wasp got what he wanted, he had carved out a section almost as big as himself and flew away with it. My local had a big laugh at me sharing my meal with a bug. I thought it was very interesting to watch him carve up that chicken.

I gave the leftovers to my local and he went to throw them away just as the wasp came back for seconds. I don't think he could tell that I no longer had anything left, and he wouldn't leave me alone. My fingers still smelled like chicken so before he decided to carve off a piece of me and fly off with it, I ran and washed my hands. I would have probably made him sick anyway.

While I'm on the subject of bugs, I had a brief encounter with an Afghan scorpion. It was just starting to turn dark and cool off, and that's when the scorpions tend to come out. He came out from the side of the road and stared me down. I say it was a brief encounter because I ran over him with my truck. He was brave to the end though.

Charles

38

the flight line

I was given a new truck to drive yesterday. I handled it as any grown man would. I grinned at the boss and said OK, no problem, I can handle it. Then I went out of sight looking for something to kick. The problem is there isn't much out here that I can kick that wouldn't kick back, so I slunk off to my new truck and went to work.

The truck I have now is a little truck that only holds three thousand gallons of water. The Mammut I was driving held ten thousand gallons. Someone said I had been demoted, but I corrected them by saying, "No, I have been de-Mammuted."

Remember the guy I said earned the right to be called my friend because he shared a steak and lobster meal with me? Well, Robbin went home for R&R for two weeks, and it is his truck and route I have been stuck with. I half suspect he was just buttering me up with that steak and lobster because he already knew I was going to be the one picked to do his route. Time will tell. He is still my friend but not such a good friend that I won't put something dead in his bed for the two weeks he is gone.

It's not all bad—this route I'm on now has me out on the flight line all day. I'm up close enough to touch the planes that most people only see in the news or movies.

My wife is going to send me a digital camera so I can start taking pictures to add to my stories. It would make things more interesting with photos to go along with them.

There are many different types of planes here, but I will describe only the ones I have learned a little about.

There are more F-15 fighter jets here than anything else except the Black Hawk helicopters.

The F-15 can fly up to 1,875 mph. That means the pilot could leave Seattle, Washington, and be over New York City in about an hour and a half. A better way of realizing what kind of speed we are talking about is to look at a shorter distance, such as from Houston, Texas, to Dallas, Texas. It would only take about eight minutes. Cool, huh?

Just think—this is not even the fastest Fighter the military has, but there is nothing here that can compete with it, I assure you. No matter where I am on the base, when these planes take off or come in for a landing, everyone stops whatever it is they are doing for a moment to watch them.

The F-15 fighters always leave in pairs and when they do take off it is with the afterburners so the plane can reach a high speed and altitude quickly.

One day we noticed only one plane take off, which is not the norm. We speculated that if he left without waiting for his partner, then he was on a mission where air support was in dire need.

A few minutes went by and then we heard a noise from the flight light, which I had never heard before. It was loud and getting louder by the second. I was not sure what it was and was afraid something had gone horribly wrong and something was about to blow up. The ground was vibrating, the buildings were shaking, things were falling from shelves, and even the rocks on the ground were bouncing like the vibrating football game board I had when I was a young boy.

Seriously, this was the most frightening thing I have experienced since I have been on the ground here. All of a sudden the second F-15 came ripping off the flight line so low and so fast we could feel the pressure in the air. Just as he cleared the end of the runway where our trucks were parked, the pilot turned the nose of his plane straight up like a rocket, causing the force of the afterburners to throw so much dust into the air we couldn't see anything for several minutes. But we defiantly heard and felt the atmosphere rip and slam back together as the pilot took his plane through the sound barrier in an effort to close the gap with the first plane.

I always thought when these planes took off with the afterburners on, they were taking off at full throttle but I learned on this day that if these planes took off at full throttle, they would shake the entire base and surrounding villages into dust.

Every night when the F-15s take off, I am close enough to see the pilot. When this airplane takes off, it has a blue-white afterburner flame about forty feet long. It is awesome.

Anyway, I have to learn this new route. I can do it but it is overwhelming. This is the only truck to haul water to the whole flight line and like I said it only holds three thousand gallons of water.

I am the low man on the totem pole and I have to learn the routes of all the drivers here just like they did when they first got here (with the exception of Robbin—hmmm, something for me to look in to).

Well, it is already late and I'm starting to doze so I better get this out. Thanks for being part of my newsletter. It does help me get through the day looking forward to writing something that might make someone smile.

Charles

39

big problem

I have been working on the flight line for four days now. I rode with the regular flight line driver for one day before he left for R&R. I rode with his local Afghan citizen for two days trying to learn the route.

It became apparent real quick that Robbin's local helper thought he could take advantage of my ignorance. He knew where all the tanks were that needed to be filled, but he was having me fill the tanks that required the least amount of work for him.

I am not opposed to finding an easier way of doing a job as long as it gets done, but what he was doing was arranging the day to suit his nap time. I couldn't keep him awake! I asked if he had gotten any sleep the night before and he said yes but "it too much hot, make tired me." I don't think he pulled that kind of stunt with Robbin. I always saw Robbin on his butt and now I know why.

I cured my own problem. I went in this morning and told the boss I could figure out the route on my own and I wanted my regular helper back. He said fine, so I collected Broder and went to work.

I was feeling good about having my guy back with me and he was grinning ear to ear as we were trucking down the taxi way when I looked to the left just in time to see a big plane about to run over us. I burned through them European truck gears like I was in a stock-car race running from that plane. I've done some stupid stuff before, but I've never taken on a C-130 with a water truck before. It took about thirty minutes for my heart to slow down. What little English my helper knew came out in two words, over and over: "Big Problem! Big Problem!"

I will be glad when Robbin comes back, and he can have the flight line back.

I haven't mentioned the guys who I have as regular helpers yet. I talked about the first guy I had assigned to me, but I think he is a bit touched in the head. The guys I have now, and have had for almost a month, are Broder and Popal.

Broder is my morning helper and Popal is my afternoon helper. I am teaching Broder English and he teaches me Farsi. I should say he is trying to teach me Farsi.

Normally a person is not aware of any accent they speak with, and I am no exception. It always surprises me when someone says I speak with an accent because I don't hear it. Well, I busted up laughing when I realized Broder is pronouncing the words he is learning just the way he hears me speak them. I now have an Afghan citizen talking with a southern drawl. I guess you would have to be here to find the humor in it but take my word, to hear him saying, "Mornin Y'all," is funny.

Popal is kind of my project. I take notes on a lot of what he says and am saving them in order to put together an orderly and informative letter just about him and his family. Popal is my helper, but his father is chief of his village. Popal reminds me of some quiet Arab prince who has dressed down to mingle with his people without being recognized. That is not really the case, but I have a story to tell about him later.

OK, I'm off to sleep and try to start the day tomorrow refreshed and more alert to planes that might be in my way.

Charles

40

FBI – CIA.

I wonder why the FBI is here. I can only guess they may be here following up leads on the cowardly 9/11 terrorist attack.

I see the FBI and the CIA agents every day. They do not mingle with anyone at all that I can tell. These agents go in and out of the prison that does not exist here, but I have never seen any of them talking or even eating at the DIFAC with anyone but their colleagues.

I expected the CIA to be here because they are known to run their own little wars and operations that are not supposed to be known to the public. Kind of like the prison that does not exist here.

41

the prison that does not exist

There is a building here that I drive by every day where I have to fill the water tanks that sit behind a tall fence with rows of razor wire running along the top. The building reminds me of a prison but that can't be the case because I am told there is no prison here. I guess my imagination is running away with me.

The water tanks I have to fill are very large, the largest ones on my route anyhow. I will load about twenty thousand gallons a day into these tanks. That amount of water is strange because I only see about fifty FBI and CIA agents and about the same amount of military personnel coming and going. That amount of water indicates a whole lot more people, but hey, what am I thinking? It must be something else, of course, and I need to get the crazy notion out of my head that there is a prison here.

One funny thing I have noticed about this building is how the inmates . . . I mean people who would look like inmates if this were really a prison . . . all enjoy their smoke and coffee break at the same time. Then again, this might be a private school. Yeah, that must be it because all of the prisoners . . . er, students . . . are all wearing the same private-school uniform. Bright orange jumpsuits.

These students play volleyball several times a day during their recess periods, and let me tell you something—these teachers at this private school are on high alert when the kids are out playing. I even see the teachers . . . very heavily armed teachers . . . walking around on top of the roof and high balconies watching for would-be kidnappers, I guess.

It still looks like a prison to me though.

42

black water?

Is it black water? I don't know.

Black water from what I understand is a private security company that is being employed in both Iraq and Afghanistan. Some might call them soldiers of fortune.

At the farthest distance you can be from the main body of military aircraft and yet still be on the flight line are a couple of hangars that house several aircraft, which only come outside when it is time to load up and fly.

I was filling one of their tanks one day when one of the planes was pushed out of the hangar. Shortly after the plane was started, a short bus arrived and ten or twelve people got off and ran for the plane. The tail section on the plane had a door. When opened, it could hold a jeep or other cargo.

The tail door was open and the men ran up the ramp even as the plane started moving. The plane has a bunch of skulls and crossbones painted on the side of it, indicating successful missions, I assume.

The men were heavily armed, and many boxes and crates were already on the plane. Some of these guys had beards and all looked like they enjoyed their job. I don't know who they are, but I know they are operating on their own agenda. I wonder if this is part of why the FBI and CIA are here.

43

rocket attack

We had a rocket attack last night. I heard the explosion and the return fire, but I just rolled over and went back to sleep.

This morning the guys working the night-shift were talking about it. They said they saw the rocket or rather the flame from the rocket as it arced over into the base. Everybody spent about two hours in the bunkers, which is where I was supposed to be.

These people are crazy to attack this base. You could not imagine the firepower the military has here. I can understand the bad guys trying to hit a small outpost but not here.

We do know they are crazy because right around the time they fired a rocket at us (I don't know how many so I'm guessing just one) they had a suicide car bomber kill forty people in Kabul just down the road a ways.

During the summer months the attacks are frequent enough, but when the first snow falls the bad guys run back through the mountain passes and it is quiet for the winter. When it snows here, it closes all access from the mountains.

Other than that bit of news it has been quite boring, day after day doing the same old thing. The days seem to go by pretty quick, though I think the nights go by faster. No sooner do I close my eyes than it is time to do it all over again.

Charles

44

popal & broder

Not a whole lot to tell anymore. If I were traveling around seeing different things and having new experiences I'm sure I could whip out all the letters I wanted. Here I just drive around and deliver water and see the same old things day after day.

There a few humorous stories I will go ahead and get out of the way. As I said in a previous update I have resorted to torturing my local helpers for sport. I have both of them scared all the time, wondering what I'm going to do to them next.

I don't hurt them and wouldn't let them get hurt and they are good sports. It helps my day go by faster.

First you have to understand the mentality of the local population. These people are not dumb and in many ways smarter than we are because they grew up and live in this hostile environment with relative ease, as opposed to a bunch of overfed foreigners trying to make it more comfortable.

The mentality that I witness with my two guys is almost childlike. I can't speak for anyone else except the two that I work with everyday.

Popal is definitely a more refined gentleman than most men I know. He is smart and goes to school every day with the ambition of becoming a doctor one day. He makes $7 a day. I asked about getting him a raise and starting on September 6 he will start earning $8.50 a day. His future is not for me to see, I guess, because I have no idea how he will make his wish come true.

Broder is as eager to please me as . . . well, I am at a loss for how to describe it. He has taken to me like he needs my approval and he needs me to tell him how good he is doing. He is his own man but he acts like he is my man.

Broder is learning English very well and he teaches me Farsi. He has a child's paperback schoolbook that he brings to work with him without fail as well as a notepad in which I write English words and he then writes the equivalent in Farsi beside them. The child's book is so worn that today he had to take some duct tape to try and make it stay together. My wife is sending him some children's books with pictures so I can help him. He is so excited to see me every day it makes me laugh.

Well, I almost forgot how I started this letter. I will give you an example of what I do to these guys sometimes.

One afternoon Broder and I were pumping water into a tank next to the fuel farm. Two guys were sitting in the shade of the tanks minding their own business.

I picked up about ten or twelve rocks to make a double handful and handed them to Broder. He's standing there with a grin on his face because he just knows I'm going to teach him something new about these rocks.

I picked another rock off the ground and threw it. It hit one of the fuel farm workers square in the back.

This guy jumped up to see what was going on and Broder was standing there in wonder and awe of me. He was grinning ear to ear thinking I was wonderful and a little crazy to pick a fight with this man. You could see it in his face, he couldn't wait to see what I would do next. He looked to the other guy to see what he was going to do and then he turned back to me again only to find me standing there pointing my finger at him, indicating it was he who threw the rock.

It dawned on him that he was the only person standing there with a double handful of rocks. The look on his face was priceless. He started shaking his head and backing away dropping the rocks and trying to tell the guy he didn't do it. The guy looked at me and I just shrugged my shoulders and kept right on doing what I was there to do while Broder spent the rest of the time in the truck.

Popal, poor Popal, today I had to drive a truck I had never driven before. I decided I needed a little practice pumping water with this truck before I got into any tight spots. I drove straight to the fire station. The fire station is in a wide-open area of the flight line, and normally there's nobody there to bother me.

Of course, today was the first day I have seen anybody at the fire station. About fifty or so soldiers were there. Many of them were resting on the very bag I needed to pump water into. A little voice in the back of my mind was telling me I should leave and come back later, but the voice sounded so much like my wife that I automatically ignored it. This almost turned fatal.

As I said, I did not know how to operate the pump. To make a long story short, I let quite a bit of water spill on the ground and where did that water want to go? It had the whole airfield to drain off to, but it drained right into the laps of the guys sitting by the bag. They jumped up—remember, these guys have guns and here I had just upset them. I turned the valve off while trying to hear what one soldier was shouting at me. I couldn't leave well enough alone. I had to know what this guy said to me, gun or no gun.

I handled it very diplomatically. I pointed at Popal and said if they wanted to string him up it was OK by me. Popal did not smile at all. He just backed away and got up in the truck. He wasn't sure if they were going to string him up or not. This broke the tension with the soldiers and I had them laughing in no time. Wet butts and all.

Charles

45

the french and their uniforms

The French sent a bunch of their army over here the other day. There was already quite a few but they added a bunch of new guys.

Right now I deliver water to everybody on the airfield so I got to watch them practice. The four helicopters they were using were not in operation, but the soldiers were pretending to be landing in hostile territory. They would all jump out and crouch and run to each person's designated area with their weapons pointed out from the chopper until they made a complete circle.

They were not very coordinated but hey, I guess that's why it's called practice.

The French seem to take a lot of pride in the way they dress. Their uniforms all looked like they had been tailored for a fashion runway instead of battle. When I see them walking down the sidewalk, they look like they should be carrying a bouquet of flowers instead of their dainty little guns.

It probably sounds like I don't like the French all that much. I don't.

Yesterday, after the French soldiers had had enough practice, I guess, they decided to go off base to patrol the area.

I was at an intersection trying to get through, and there they came. A big long convoy of military vehicles traveling at a high rate of speed and not bothering to slow down or stop at the intersection. The base speed limit is only 25 kph, which is about 15 mph. These guys were intent on a show of force, and they were trying to impress us on the base, I guess.

Anyway, there they came in their jungle camouflage vehicle with each soldier decked out in the latest fashion in the warfare wardrobe department. These guys had little bushes on top of their helmets and some even had vines and leaves to help camouflage their uniforms.

Well, there they went right out the gate with their jungle camouflage convoy into a desert.

I wonder if they even noticed that the US soldiers are in desert camouflage. Oh, they probably think that with a desert-tan uniform it will be harder to swoon the chicks. They can have all the chicks here they want. In a desert I would rather be dressed to look like a rock than a banana tree.

Any local bad guy would say, "Just shoot into that clump of green bushes, I bet you hit something."

OK, enough of my sarcasm. Let them share some of

the burden that our men do. I don't care if they do look like a bunch of pansies.

Charles

PS: I feel so ashamed of myself.

I wrote about the French soldiers a few days ago and started to delete the story altogether, but instead I want you to hear the rest of the story now.

The French soldiers were indeed attacked near the Pakistan border. Many soldiers died.

I was on the flight line when just about every helicopter on the base took off at the same time. I believe now they were responding to the attack on the French.

I don't know what else to say.

46
red cross

The Red Cross contacted my company today.

My dad is in the hospital with cancer and is not expected to survive more than a couple of weeks so I am going to pack a bag, lock up my room, and go home.

I hope to make it home in time.

47

the $120 haircut

Dubai again!

I've got to tell you, I don't know if I want to share this email or not because it goes against almost all the cowboy instincts I was born with.

When I say born with, it is because my belief is that a man is born to enjoy the touch of a woman, not that of another man. I believe everyone is born for the love of family regardless of male or female, but the touch of a strange man is one I think has to be learned as a person grows into life.

I have friends who have that streak in them, but it is not in me. I say cowboy instincts because I don't know many cowboys who like anything but women. The Brokeback Mountain boys don't count. They were not cowboys; they were sheep herders.

Anyway, I'm getting off my story. I felt violated again

today. Dubai again! By another man. What is it about this place?

Dubai has laws that prohibit making public displays of affection between a man and a woman, including husband and wife. There are no holding hands or kisses in public. I thought this would make the perfect getaway for my wife and me.

I am in a hotel called the Grand. It is nice but just like the last time I am sharing a room with another man. I knocked on the door two times before I opened it this time. A big black guy was about to open the door when I opened it. He was confused as to why I knocked till I explained about the last time I discovered a naked man in the room and even after closing the door to allow him time to get clothed or hide he was still there when I opened the door. My new roommate laughed and said he understood, and that he would keep his clothes on.

It took me thirty-six hours to get here from the time I woke up at home so I was tired by the time I actually got to bed again. The room is pretty much like it was before. I know how to make the water heater and air conditioner work and learned the trick to keep the water and Stuff from backing up onto the bathroom floor.

To get to my story, I have to say I slept hard and didn't get up till 2:00 p.m. Of course that would be 4:30 a.m. back home so my body is still on Texas time.

I have to attend a 5:30 p.m. meeting tonight to find out when I fly out to Afghanistan. I had some time to kill so I walked around the hotel gift shops thinking I might buy my wife a gift when I spotted a barber.

OK, now it sounds like I'm contradicting myself here but I'm not. A barber does not count when it comes to being touched by another man. Most barbers.

I like what is called a high-and-tight haircut. Women do not know how to give a high-and-tight haircut and I think it is because all women have this gene that will not allow them to grasp a barber sheer and just buzz a man's head to chop off his hair in about two minutes and take his $5 so he can go on about his business with a fresh, short haircut feeling good about himself.

I walked in knowing I was making a mistake because I had already noticed there was no red, white, and blue barber pole advertising this place of business. Oh well.

I was walking through the gift shops, like I said, when I spotted a barber. A man barber. I saw he had all the buzz tools for a good high-and-tight and even had the whisker broom and straight razor for a shave. I was so excited about the prospect of a haircut and a shave that I didn't consider the fact that a straight razor to my throat in an Arab country might not be the smartest thing I've allowed to happen to me.

I'm getting ahead of myself again.

I have to point out that the barber could not speak English but hey, he had all the tools I knew he needed for a high-and-tight so I just smiled and sat down. We both made hand gestures and pulled our hair until he was certain he knew what I wanted and I was certain

I was getting a high-and-tight. Oh yeah, we agreed I both needed and wanted a hot shave. Man, this was going to be heaven.

I sat down; he broke out the sheet and put it on me. Here came the little choke strap made out of extra-strength toilet paper. We were on track so far. Yes, here came the buzzing tool and my non-English-speaking barber went to work.

He finished with the buzzers a little sooner than I thought he should, but he let me know. No problem. My barber broke from the normal procedure of a high-and-tight by grabbing some scissors. This is where most of the women barbers start, with a pair of scissors. Have you ever met a pair of scissors that were actually designed to fit a man's hand? Me neither.

My barber used the scissors very skillfully. I qualify this statement by the fact that he did not draw blood. He pulled the hair on top of my head between his fingers and asked me if another barber left it in such a shambles. He just shook his head and started trimming it to his satisfaction.

The haircut was finished. I was not sure if he was done because I did not yet have a high-and-tight. When the barber took a blow-dryer to my head and then combed in some hair gel I was sure he was done. The finished product looked a lot like it did when I first sat down.

Here came the barber with the hot lather for my shave and I forgot about the high-and-tight. There is something about a hot shave that makes a bad haircut acceptable.

Man, that shave was feeling good till he paused on my neck just long enough for me to realize I might be in trouble. No problem. This seems to be a favorite American saying in this part of the world. The barber took this moment to bring me a box to look at. It was a box containing something in little bottles, but I had no idea what it was. He said to read the back of the box. I did.

I said I had no need for any product to stop my hair from falling out. The barber disagreed with me and used hand signals and spoke some gibberish that sounded like the language I hear coming out of my wife's mouth when she says I'm going bald.

I said "I didn't care if all my hair fell out, so I don't need your product, thank you." The barber looked at my hair with what I believe to be disgust, then reached up and grabbed an off-color hair and pulled it out of my head. Guess what? Now he wanted to add color to my hair. I said what for? I don't have gray hair. He pulled a second hair out of my head and insisted I was in dire need of some help. I told him he would be in dire need of help if he pulled another hair out of my head. I think he understood more English than he had been letting on because he went back to shaving me.

The shave was done. It was very nice and you would think my visit would be over but wait, there is more.

The barber was cleaning up the shaving lotion with some small towels with aftershave on them. He was cleaning with those little towels when all of a sudden he grabbed the end of my nose and mashed it so hard to one side I thought he was going to break it.

I know you're probably thinking the very thoughts that were running through my own head and which I was just about to react upon when he grabbed it a second time and mashed it the other way, kind of like he was trying to bend it back into place.

Through the tears in my eyes I could see him looking at my nose very closely with a nasty look of disgust, and in fact he was saying to me, "Disgusting." I was wondering if he mashed a big bugger that had been hiding in there somewhere, making it come out to surrender when he brought me a mirror.

What he had done was mash my nose hard enough to cause some of the pores to evacuate. OK, so he mashed hard enough to make the oil and dirt pop up out of their hiding place in the skin of my nose. He said, "I fix, no problem." Of course I agreed. I didn't want to walk out with a big swollen nose when all I wanted was a high-and-tight. I said, "Fix it."

Here he came with some cream that felt like Goop, the hand cleaner with the pumice in it. I knew what he was going to do before he did it. He used that pumice-filled cream to scrub my face off.

I was beginning to think this guy might not be a barber at all. At the same time I was beginning to have a whole new respect for a woman's pain threshold. The only reason I didn't jump up and a quit this thing is because I didn't know what would be more embarrassing—getting a facial or admitting I wasn't man enough to handle the pain of a facial.

The scrub was only the beginning. Here he came again with some more cream. This cream took some of the sting out of my face and I was thinking it might be OK now. Wrong!

He left the cream on my face and then rolled a steamer over to me, so now I was smothering to death with this cream on my face and only a small area to breathe from. This steamer did two things. One, it made the smoothing cream very hot (not fun), and two, it cut off the only relief I had—the blowhole I was breathing through. Torture!

OK, I'm getting to the end of my ordeal.

The Sweeny Todd of Dubai scrubbed what was left of my face off and gave me a mirror. He said with a smile, "GOOD!?" I was afraid to say no so I said, "Good," but without enthusiasm. I thought the pain was over.

He held out his hand and wanted $120.

I'm sitting in the dark of my hotel room writing this, feeling violated. My face does not move. I can't smile or frown and I don't want to talk to anybody for fear I don't have enough oil left in my face for my lips to form the words.

If I ever go through that again, I would just as soon want it to be a woman who tortures me. Still no streak there.

All I wanted was a high-and-tight.

Charles

48

home for a time

I am home and I wish I could say it is an enjoyable trip.

It is nice to see family and friends, but nobody likes to come together for an illness or death. Nobody wants or enjoys it when it comes time to say good-bye.

I was with my dad the day he found out he had cancer and he took the news in stride. He simply said God had healed him after having a heart attack and then again when he recovered from colon cancer, so lung cancer should not be anything to worry about.

I watched as my dad started losing weight and strength. He started asking me to do things that I know just about killed him to have to ask because in his mind he was still strong physically. My mom, Dottie, has always been a very strong person and that is what kept my dad around as long as he was. He was determined to win one more argument.

He and my mom would get into a verbal jousting match and then Mom would get fed up and go into the kitchen and Dad would look at me and wink with a mischievous grin on his face, declaring the battle won.

My dad still believes he is going to be God's miracle. I believe it, too. Even if I had doubts, Dad's spirit and conviction have dispelled them.

It is nearing the time I have to go back to work. Do I go with my mom here alone with Dad being so weak?

Every day I have been home, Dad seems to have gotten stronger. He is more animated and even eating more and gaining strength. Mom assures me she has everything under control if I need to return to work.

Dad says again he knows he is going to be another miracle and that I should go.

49

frankfurt, germany, gate b-20

I am back in Dubai at the time I'm writing this. I think I will just stay hidden in my hotel room until it is time to fly out to Bagram. I can't afford any more Dubai surprises or high-and-tights here.

I had to fly through Frankfurt, Germany, to get this far into my journey and after a six-hour layover there, I have something to write about.

Now you have to take my summary of the whole German population with a grain of salt, considering my whole experience with the country came from Terminal B, Frankfurt airport, Gate B-20.

When traveling abroad—and no, I'm not talking about when my wife goes to visit her mother, I'm talking about when you leave the United States of America in your travels—you get to rub shoulders with many cultures we only see in the pages of National Geographic.

If there is one place that tries to accommodate all

cultures at the same time it is an international airport. As a police officer I had to take a mandatory cultural diversity course every couple of years. One trip to an international airport for the purpose of observing the masses has a much greater impact than any classroom.

Before I get to my German story, the one thing I have noticed in every country I have been in so far is that the Arab or Middle Eastern people, especially the women, are rude, arrogant, and have no respect for personal space, until I educate them. As a whole I can't do much about it, but I make my displeasure known to the ones who like to bump into me from behind with their luggage cart or constantly bump into my back-pack while I'm in line to get somewhere and especially those who think it is OK for their family of fifteen to cut into the line because they don't want to be behind a lone infidel. I must have an awful meaningful look in my eye when I make them aware of the problem I have with their actions. It may get me locked up one day, but if I'm not in their country I don't let them get away with it. In their country I let them do what they want if I want to keep both ears on my head.

I am ashamed to say that yesterday it was the American who I found to be distasteful. Hehe . . . sounds like I'm a restaurant critic.

I was in line to get my boarding pass in Frankfurt. Everybody was being nice and quiet while waiting their turn except one person just ahead of me. Well, the guy right in front of me was a small Indian man trying to keep to himself, but the one in front of him was a big boy from America. This kid was about six feet tall and looked like he probably had been in good shape while going to high school. But not anymore. He was still big but quickly turning to lard.

This big guy from America . . . I hate saying that because he was so embarrassing. He was wearing the brightest green pullover shirt I have ever seen that had the word "Irish" emblazoned across the chest. I don't care what he wanted to wear, but every time he opened his mouth something loud and stupid would come out. People who can't help but say stupid things while in public certainly don't need to be issued passports. Hmmm . . . I almost didn't get one, what's up with that?

Every couple of minutes this guy would say, "Look at that Mormon over there, he just keeps walking back and forth and back and forth, look at him." Everybody in the line would turn and look because he was so loud. The big guy turned to the Indian in front of me and practically yelled at him to look at that Mormon. When the Indian fellow did as he was told, the big guy said again, "Keep looking, that Mormon is hiding behind that pole there."

I had already seen what he was talking about and after the third time of him trying to get everybody to look at that Mormon I had to correct him. I did so in a much more moderate voice. "I believe, sir, you are seeing a Jewish rabbi and his family. I don't think he is doing anything wrong, it will be OK."

The big guy just looked at me, dumbfounded; it took a moment to sink in that everything would be alright. He said, "OK, well I'm going to get me some German food while I'm here, you know being in Germany and all. I want some real German food."

This was an abrupt change in his thought process. If he were capable of having more than one thought at a time he might have just eaten that Jewish rabbi and told everybody how good that Mormon tasted.

That was a side story to the one I want to relay to you.

German people don't seem to have a sense of humor. Remember I'm talking about the ones I saw in the airport.

What I saw were a people working in a very methodical manner. There was no horseplay and every person had their job to do, and they did it over and over again. What I saw in the work habits of the German employees was not what I was used to in the United States. We get the job done in the United States, but no job gets done without a little horseplay or joking around with one another. As a matter of fact if I can't cut up and have fun while on the job, I will find another job. Germany is a different culture.

None of the German workers were rude; they just did their job thoroughly and seemingly without complaint. The Germans are more thorough in their screening process than I have seen anywhere else. It kind of made me feel safer. I had already formed my opinion of these German workers before I saw what I am about to tell you.

How long has it been since the Twin Towers were knocked down? Eight years? How many billions of times have you heard that certain items were not going to be allowed on an airplane, such as knives, box cutters, such and such?

I had a long layover and nowhere to sit. I was wandering around the terminal when I spotted an empty chair near Gate B-20. I sat and found myself right behind the guy looking at the X-ray images of carry-on baggage for the flight out of that gate going to Washington D.C.

That was a cool machine he was working with. It showed him everything in the bags. Most bags have multiple layers and the machine shows each layer in a different color. The operator just goes to the color he wants to look at and all others disappear, allowing him to see what is in the bag. He can look at each layer separately. Pretty cool.

One of the layers showed an item the operator did not like. He called another screener over to open the bag and found a knife. Yes, a knife in a carry-on bag for a plane going to Washington D.C.

I am ashamed to admit it, but this bag belonged to an American. What an idiot. I was wishing the other loud, hungry American would come along and eat this guy.

Remember when I said the German people did not seem to have a sense of humor?

This guy was trying to blow it off as a mistake, and he just wanted to get on the plane. He thought they should have just kept the knife and let him go. That's not what happened. He should have been publicly flogged but that didn't happen either. What the Germans did to him was far worse.

While all the other passengers filed by him getting on the plane, our knife-baring friend had to stand there. Every one of his fellow passengers going by him looked at him like he was the scum of the earth, the next Shoe Bomber. I couldn't help but laugh at him. He caught me a couple of times and I know he wanted to strangle me, but that would just add to his problems. Can you imagine being put on ice for trying to board a plane with a knife, only to be caught moments later trying to choke someone to death? That thought made me laugh even more.

While he was standing there, the guy started to worry that he might not get on the plane and started to get frustrated. He told the screener to keep the knife and he would just get on the plane, but before he could walk off, the screener grabbed him and said he was to stay put. A few seconds later an airport official showed up, talked to the man for a second, took the knife, and left.

I needed to go check on my own flight, but I didn't want to miss the end of this real-life drama, so I waited. The guy was really getting antsy about missing his ride to Washington, and I was almost as antsy because I didn't want to miss my flight to Dubai.

Our guy was pacing back and forth, back and forth, like the Mormon-rabbi. I wonder now if they were both just praying for a plane to get on. He would stop every few seconds and look at the people getting on the plane and just do a little frustrated dance that made me laugh every time. This guy was miserable and I was enjoying it. I normally don't find pleasure in other people's misery but I am so scared of flying as it is I would have voted to hang this guy in the middle of the terminal as a warning to any real terrorist. You string an idiot or two up by mistake and the real thing may never happen again.

The German police finally showed up and I saw this guy just melting in his shoes. All the arrogance left him at once; he thought he was going to jail. As it was, the cop had a lot of paperwork to do and it was taking a long time to do it. Was this guy going to make his flight? Was I?

Yes, he made his flight by mere seconds and I can only imagine the looks he got from everyone onboard. He was the last one to get on the plane. How many times he was called and idiot I couldn't tell you, but I'm sure it was a long flight home for him.

When the man finally got to leave, the cop put the knife in his own pocket and the Germans started to laugh and to cut up with one another . . . hmmm, maybe the German people have a sense of humor, after all.

I made my flight, too. I am hiding out in my hotel room in Dubai.

Charles

50

red cross again

I was just minutes from catching my flight to Bagram, Afghanistan, when the Red Cross managed to get a message to me. Dad was gone.

The Red Cross is an amazing group of people.

I am eighteen hours flying time from home. It is going to be a long trip.

Coming Home to Say Good-bye

I am home again. Man, what a stressful month this has been. Everyone is together again.

I don't know why I left. I wonder if Dad would have continued to gain strength and recover if I had stayed home. I know I had nothing to do with his health, good or bad, but I still wonder.

Every day I have been home, my extended family in Bagram has been sending me emails and making expensive international phone calls to check on me and my family. What a great bunch of guys I work with.

Back to Bagram Airfield, Afghanistan

I could stay home, but I find myself preparing to leave again for Afghanistan. If I stay home I will violate the agreement in the contract I made with my employer.

If I break the contract, I will not be eligible to work for them again.

The good thing is that if I go back to Bagram, Afghanistan, I can terminate my employment and will be eligible to go back to work again after a four-month leave of absence.

It doesn't make sense to me because of the expense involved in flying me to Afghanistan and then all the way back to Texas.

It doesn't make sense but I know why they do it. The company actually loses money if I stay home. If I am back in Dubai, Kuwait, Iraq, or Afghanistan, the US government will pay the bill for my flight and pay the company for me being there.

51

fallen comrade flag

"We shall never forget and we shall avenge thee."

This is what it says at the bottom of the certificate.

I made it back to Bagram Airfield, Afghanistan, OK and the guys met me with cheers and claps on the back. I am glad to be back, but at the same time I had to let them all know I am not going to stay long. I have made up my mind to come home.

I feel like the time for me to be closer to home has come. I have been away for four years now. Not all of that time was spent in Afghanistan, but away from home still means that you are not home no matter where you are.

King Richard waited until the end of the workday and then stopped by my B-Hut to drop a gift off.

The King is a great person. While I was away because of my Dad's sickness and subsequent death, he was checking on me every day.

When I returned, he gave me a handmade wooden shadow box containing a US flag and certificate of authenticity.

King Richard is friends with people in several of the different camps here at the base. I'm sorry I don't know which group of guys it was who built the shadow box, but I am grateful. These men made the box for me when King Richard told them what he needed it for.

The US flag was flown over Camp Vance and this is what the certificate says . . .

> *This certifies that the accompanying United States Flag was flown at the Combined Joint Special Operations Task Force-Afghanistan, Camp Vance Compound on Bagram Airfield, Afghanistan*
>
> *on 15 August 2008 during*
> *Operation Enduring Freedom*
> *In Honor of*
> *Benny E. Holt*
>
> *"We shall never forget and we shall avenge thee"*
>
> *Benny E. Holt died August 15, 2008*
>
> *Thank you Richard Mills, aka King Richard, and God bless our troops. Thank you all.*

52

the final chapter, thank you

I have come to the end of my visit and my story. I hope you have enjoyed my stories as much as I have enjoyed telling them to you.

I will leave the hardest ones for me to write till the very end. I will have to break the news of my decision to leave Afghanistan to Popal and Broder in the morning.

A Wedding Gift for Popal

Popal wants to get married. The whole time I have been here, this is his favorite topic. When he talks about the girl he loves, his face brightens and there is a pep in his step that I can see.

Popal has a problem because he will have to purchase his girlfriend from her father if he is to marry her. Love doesn't pay the bills and if another man pays the price before Popal can, then his love will be lost to him.

There are not many in this part of Afghanistan wealthy enough to purchase her, but still . . .

Popal has been working for the last two years for the money, and at the rate he is going it will be another two years before he can marry her. He is so excited, only two more years.

The money is only part of the price. Popal is required to bake her father two hundred bricks and provide him with twenty goats and so many baskets of various garden vegetables.

I gave Popal the two-years salary he needed for his wedding. On the condition that it took place before I left Afghanistan.

The local villagers came together and half of the guys who should have been to work didn't show up because of the wedding.

I could not go, of course, but the look in Popal's eyes and the tremor in his voice when he asked me, "You would do this for me?" were enough.

Popal brought me a gift from his father with an invitation to meet with him should a chance ever arise. He also brought me several gifts from his party, such as candies and fruit. The last thing he gave me was a white scarf that his new wife made out of her wedding dress. She had sewn a message of thanks and love and gave the only thing she had of value to me, a piece of the material taken from her dress.

Tears of Popal and Broder

Popal cried and said he was going to miss me. He worked a little slower the last few days I was there, and it seemed like he was trying to make the time last a little longer.

I felt bad and sometimes even guilty that I was leaving him, but everything was already in place to ship back home. I wished Popal the happiest marriage and made sure he was getting his raise.

Broder is a little harder to deal with. Broder cried like a baby until I cried myself.

Broder is very kindhearted, and I think he was a little broken when I told him I was leaving. He begged me not to go and then begged me to take him with me. He wanted nothing else than to work for me from now on.

I tried to tell him it just was not possible, and let me tell you it hurt as much as if I were giving up my only child for adoption.

I asked Robbin if he would take on the proper care and nourishment of Broder, and he said he would be honored. All of the drivers have gone through several different helpers during the time I have had Popal and Broder. I guess I just got lucky to have two great guys to work with.

Popal and Broder may be in the group of people who have to be monitored at all times for signs of malice, but there is no malice in them. Both men wear their feelings on their shoulders. One with the air of compassionate royalty, and the other with the inno-cence of a child.

These men are my friends and getting to know them has enriched my life. I hope to see you again,

Charles